ALLISON MOORE
with Nancy Woodruff

SHARDS

A Young Vice Cop Investigates Her Darkest

Case of Meth Addiction—Her Own

Touchstone

New York   London   Toronto   Sydney   New Delhi

Touchstone
An Imprint of Simon & Schuster, Inc.
1230 Avenue of the Americas
New York, NY 10020

First Touchstone trade paperback edition April 2015

TOUCHSTONE and colophon are registered trademarks of Simon & Schuster, Inc.

For information about special discounts for bulk purchases, please contact Simon & Schuster Special Sales at 1-866-506-1949 or business@simonandschuster.com.

The Simon & Schuster Speakers Bureau can bring authors to your live event. For more information or to book an event contact the Simon & Schuster Speakers Bureau at 1-866-248-3049 or visit our website at www.simonspeakers.com.

Interior design by Akasha Archer

Manufactured in the United States of America

10 9 8 7 6 5 4 3 2 1

The Library of Congress has cataloged the hardcover edition as follows:

Moore, Allison, 1981–
    Shards / Allison Moore with Nancy Woodruff.
        pages cm
    "A Touchstone book."
    1. Moore, Allison, 1981– 2. Police—Hawaii—Maui—Biography. 3. Vice control—Hawaii—Maui. 4. Police—Drug use—Hawaii—Maui. I. Title.
    HV7911.M647A3 2014
    363.2092—dc23
    [B]
                                                            2013026028

ISBN 978-1-4516-9635-6
ISBN 978-1-4516-9636-3 (pbk)
ISBN 978-1-4516-9637-0 (ebook)

For my family

SHARDS

Prologue

He wants to take a shower so I make it ready for him, turning the stiff chrome handle until the water is perfect.

Everything, everything has to be perfect for him. *If he doesn't like the temperature of the water. If I add too much cream to his coffee. If I don't weigh exactly 116 pounds.*

The consequences are never the same. I would love to know that when I fuck up I will just get the shit kicked out of me, but every time is different. Sometimes it's just a beating. Sometimes I have to face the wall while he whips me with a rubber hose. Other times, my head in the toilet until I can't breathe. Or this: brushing my teeth with Mechanics hand cleaner while he grabs my throat so I can't swallow.

This time I am careful not to fuck up. I only need a few minutes. Just enough time to go downstairs for the gun. Most of the weapons have been hidden away except for the revolver he keeps in the shop for protection. He never sells from the house, but sometimes he'll negotiate there.

He has a name, but I can't speak or even spell it. I'll call him my dealer.

While he's in the shower, my job is to get his clothes ready, make his coffee, load a bowl with dope, bring everything into the bathroom, and stay there until he is ready to get out.

But not today. Not today.

My plan is to kill him, then kill myself. I'll get him coming out of the shower.

I walk down the stairs and go into the shop. I don't know if it's morning or night and I don't even care. I'm on tweaker time. I've been up for days.

The revolver is exactly where I know it is, in the back of a drawer in his worktable, in a FedEx envelope addressed to his friend Joe. A Ruger .38 with a black handle and wood inlay, disassembled.

Putting together a revolver isn't difficult, but only if I remain calm. I move into work mode. In recruit school we had this saying: *slow is smooth and smooth is fast*. If you're trying to rush putting a mag in your firearm you'll fumble it up. If you take your time it goes faster in the end.

I insert the cylinder, then the trigger guard, steady, thinking clearly. I'm not shaking. Except for my hands, I'm completely still, focusing so hard on listening. I can still hear the shower going, the water running through the pipes down to the basement.

I've thought about leaving a note for my family, for Keawe, but I have been too scared the dealer would find it or see me writing it. For me there are no hiding places in this house, no secrets from him. I figure I can write to the people I love after I kill him, before I kill myself. I have thought a lot about what I want to write, but all I can really say is that I love them, and that I'm sorry. I'm not going to try to explain anything. There is no explanation for what I have done and what has been done to me. Just *Sorry* and *I love you*, that's all.

Will they ever see the note? Who will even find us—the dealer's friend Joe or one of his drug groupies? Will they bother to call the cops?

How will they even know who I am?

I push these thoughts away. I need to stay focused. *Slow is smooth, smooth is fast.* I insert the hammer and the hammer pin, then the spring. I have a little trouble with the spring, but it doesn't faze me. The handle, the wood inlays, then the pin that you push in to hold it all together. Once I put the inlays in I grab the last piece, a screw that holds the inlays and the handle together.

The shower stops. I should be there with his clothes, his coffee, the bowl of dope. In a minute he'll come looking for me, but it's okay. I'll get him coming down the stairs.

I cannot change my mind now, and I don't want to. In my heart I know I will die in this house. I want to die. I want to take him with me, but if there's only one bullet, I'll use it on myself.

I have to finish turning the screw—I have no tools, so it's going slow. I want to load the gun first. I look up from what I'm doing, shaking the envelope.

I can't find the bullets.

There are no bullets.

He's the master of hidden compartments—meth in the hollowed-out leg of his kitchen table, coke in the recessed lighting. If there are bullets, they could be anywhere, and I don't have enough time.

My body collapses. I tell myself, *You have to move, because when he gets out of the shower he's going to come looking for you.*

I look wildly around the shop for tools I can kill him with, but he's taken everything dangerous from the house, even the kitchen knives. He knows I want to die. I have told him so over and over again.

Even if I do manage to kill him now, how will I find a way to die?

My hands no longer steady, I start to disassemble the gun, to put the parts back in the envelope and into the drawer before he gets to the shop. But he'll know anyway. There are cameras hidden all over the house, in every corner of every room, in the recessed lighting, the air vents, the electrical sockets. If he watches the footage he'll know what I was trying to do.

Slow is smooth and smooth is fast. I'm rushing now, I'm fucking it up. I need a hit.

His footsteps on the stairs—I hear them.

He's coming down now, to find me.

I'm living in hell and I can't even die.

1

I never intended to become a cop.

To be honest, it had never crossed my mind.

Growing up, I adored soccer and always wanted to go pro. That was my little girl dream, my teenage dream even, but once I let it die, I didn't bother to replace it with anything else. After high school, I took off, first going on the road with my motocross boyfriend, Vin, and then drifting between my hometown of Albuquerque and where my sister lived in Seattle. After a broken engagement to a high school basketball coach, I settled in Maui, taking science classes at the community college until I determined I wasn't going to make it as a premed.

I loved Maui. My family had spent summers and Christmases there during what I look back on as my perfect childhood—before my dad left us; before my mom started drinking; and before my sister got into the car accident that would cost her a leg. I felt embraced by the friendliness and openness of Hawaiian people. All my life I had held people at arm's length, throwing myself full-force into anything—soccer, anorexia, obsessive relationships—that would help me forget how isolated I was. On Maui, my life felt different. Now I needed a purpose, a way to make an impact on the Hawaiian community I had grown to love. I saw an ad in the newspaper for the police department and, on a whim, I applied.

I didn't hear back from the department, and I forgot about it. I took a waitressing job at Lulu's in Kihei, and started to date a new boyfriend, Dalton. Starting in high school, I had had a series of long-term boyfriends, poor attempts to fill the void left in my life by my father. I felt Dalton was different. He was very Southern, very polite. A fun-loving frat boy taking a break from college. We went snorkeling and scuba diving together; we camped on the beach; on weekend nights, we built great bonfires in the sand with all of his friends around. Dalton had a lot of friends that became my friends, and he had created this life for himself that I believed was my life also. I had a terrible history with men, starting with my father, but my relationship with Dalton felt normal and healthy.

A couple of months into my relationship with Dalton, MPD contacted me, wanting me to proceed with the interview process.

I told Dalton about it one lazy afternoon at Keawakapu Beach. He worked as a pool bartender at the Grand Wailea, but it was his day off, and I didn't have to be at Lulu's until five thirty.

"You know how I'm always saying how much I want to be part of the community here?" I asked him.

"Yeah, though I can't say why." Dalton was from Miami and a bit of an East Coast snob. After just a couple of months on Maui, he had come to hate the island culture and the pidgin. He felt the locals had no education, no drive. He was ready to go back home, but he was staying because of me.

"I applied for the police department, and I've got an interview," I told him.

He laughed, and then realized I was serious.

"What? Come on, everyone hates cops."

"Not everyone. You don't hate cops. I don't hate cops."

"I'm sure it would be very easy for a blond *haole* girl to become a cop on Maui," Dalton said, condescending and sarcastic.

"Why?" I said, starting to get annoyed. "I'm smart. I work hard."

He ran his warm hand along one of my biceps. "And you're in fantastic shape, darling," he said. "You would get those lazy Hawaiian mokes off their asses."

"I think I'd love it," I said. "I never want the nine-to-five. I'm an adrenaline junkie. I just am."

"I guess you can't be a waitress forever."

"Thank you for sounding like my mom, Dalton."

I had loved waitressing at Lulu's when I started, shooting the shit with the locals, flirting with the tourists, hanging out after work with the other girls who worked there. It was a fun restaurant near the water, and many nights Dalton came in with his roommates and closed down the place. But my mom had been on my back to do something with my life, and with Dalton planning to return to Miami soon, I felt the pressure to move on.

Could I really be a police officer?

Did I stand a chance?

My mom called from Albuquerque the next morning and I didn't even tell her about it.

"So Alli," she asked, "are you signing up for any classes at MCC next semester?"

"Mmm," I said. By this time, I had concluded that college wasn't for me. I was smart enough, but I couldn't sit still in lectures and was very lazy about homework. "We'll see."

"Because I think we can come up with some money if you need it," my mom was saying. "Your grandma—"

"No, that's okay," I said, pushing her off. "I'm making good money. I'm supporting myself."

"I know you are, Alli," my mom said. "But you can't—"

Be a waitress forever.

I knew.

I went back to snorkeling and working out and getting tan and concentrating on Dalton. Unlike all the other guys I had gone out with, Dalton was a great boyfriend. A real Southern gentleman. Not a jerk. Not someone who would ever let me down.

All I'd ever wanted from Maui was a new life, completely different from my old one, and now it looked like I was going to have it.

My childhood was wonderful—soccer games, barbecues, a big and loving extended family. Fun, artsy mother, sweet older sister, and my father, Ian. My hero. My role model.

I was a daddy's girl. While my sister was into cheerleading and gymnastics and dance, I spent my childhood following my father everywhere. Whatever he did, I was by his side. I spent hours in the garage, helping him restore old hot rods. As soon as I was old enough, I started working out with him at the gym. At holidays and family gatherings, while the rest of the family chatted and cooked and did dishes together, he would take a nap on the couch and I would fall asleep beside him. My father had an uncanny ability to detach from all around him and in this, too, I tried to copy him.

My father was an architect, and he had designed and built our house. He loved vertical gray brick and put it everywhere, inside and out, adding lots of sliding glass doors, high windows, and angles. There wasn't a square room in the house. Mom, an artist, couldn't stand *not* painting and redecorating, and our house was a constant battle between the architect and the artist. She carefully painted the dining room walls to create a Tuscan feel long before that was popular. She designed abstract wire sconces for the walls. She was always sewing slipcovers and pillowcases, forever redesigning, rearranging, sanding, painting—anything she could do to create a home. The house was full of Mom's paintings, my father's photographs and woodwork, Granddad's paintings, and Grandma Mimi's pottery, almost in competition.

Things changed between my father and me when I was twelve or thirteen. *I* changed—adolescence and all that—but my father did too. He started pulling away from the family, traveling constantly, only coming home a day or two each month. He stopped inviting me to work out with him, stopped coming to my soccer games. I thought work was the reason for his distance, but when I was fourteen I found out that he had begun an affair with his secretary. Soon afterward he left us for her, and they moved into a house across town. He had moved out of our house but also out of our lives. My sister and I saw him only on rare occasions—and even then we had to arrange everything through this secretary, whom I couldn't help but hate. It was then that I threw myself into my doomed relationship with a high school boy named Josh.

The sliding glass doors that led from my bedroom into the front yard made it easy for a despondent teenager to escape from the house. I spent nights sneaking out to smoke pot and go joyriding with Josh. I gave up my other friends, my grades slipped, and I got kicked off the soccer team. My whole life telescoped down to Josh and me.

Josh was controlling and abusive. *You don't call me enough. You're not thin enough. You don't have sex with me enough.* He got into fistfights with my friends and sometimes with me.

We tortured each other.

I loved him.

Despite the fact that we were both miserable, we stayed together all through high school. I had never had a lot of girlfriends—I just wasn't good at those kinds of friendships—and now that my father was gone, I was trying to replace him with Josh.

It was only after high school ended and Josh joined the Marines that we stopped tormenting each other and I moved on to Vin and then Hal, who I eventually dumped for Maui. Now, twenty-three years old, in love with the island, I was ready to put down roots, ready to make Maui my home for the rest of my life.

I had applied to the police department on an impulse, but as I started to go through the interview process I got excited about the questions they were asking me—questions about my past, about ethics, about the way I thought. They dug way down to figure out if I would be a good candidate, and suddenly I wanted to be. It started to be important to me to be more than a waitress with a great body and a great boyfriend. I wanted to be a cop.

After each step in the process, I assumed I would get cut. But that didn't happen. Written exam: passed. Psychological test: passed. Background check: passed. The department had to go back and find a child psychiatrist my mom had taken me to see when I was fourteen and depressed because my dad had moved out. The guy had retired, but they tracked him down and got him to sign a statement saying I was mentally sound. After that, there was a polygraph test, which I also passed.

"Darling, you have to be kidding me," Dalton would say every time I advanced to the next level. It got to be a joke between us. I finally promised him I would move to Miami with him if I failed to get in.

Around this time, I was buying a soda in a 7-Eleven when a girl ran in screaming that her boyfriend was chasing her with a knife. Before anyone else had time to react, I barricaded the doors and called 911. The guy stood outside yelling and pounding on the doors until the cops came and arrested him. I loved the rush I got from taking action in such a heated situation.

At last I had only one step left: the final interview. When I walked into the room, six men in uniform stared at me—the chief, the deputy chief, three assistant chiefs, and an internal affairs detective. I could tell they thought I was a spaz. I was sure I had blown it.

It was only after the interview that I told my mom I had applied. I figured she would be happy to hear that I had tried to be something more than a waitress.

I broke it to her casually. "Do you remember when I was a kid and we saw that burglar breaking into the Andersons' house?" I asked her over the phone.

"How could I forget," she said. "I called the cops, but you went chasing after the guy before they even got there. And then I had to chase after *you*. I've never been so frightened in my life. I could have killed you."

"It seems like I have this certain instinct—"

"You were eleven!" She laughed and I could hear the ice cubes clink as her glass shook.

"But there was that time in high school too, remember?" I said. "When those kids put a dry ice bomb in the yard? I called the cops and they sent the ATF, but instead of waiting for them I went running outside to catch whoever left it."

"Yes! You went hauling out there in your pajamas and bare feet. Good thing it was just a dry ice bomb."

I hadn't even told my mom about what had happened most recently, at the 7-Eleven here on Maui.

"So," I said. "I was thinking about the way I'm . . . attracted to crime. And—I decided to apply for a job in the police department."

"What? Alli! You're kidding, right?"

"No. I'm not."

"I'm sorry, but that's way too dangerous," she said, as if that was the last word on the subject. I was touched by her concern. What mother wants her daughter to be a cop?

"It's my decision," I said. "I probably won't even get in."

News travels fast in my family. An hour later my sister called. "How are you going to yell loud enough to arrest somebody?" she asked. "How will they hear you with that little Minnie Mouse voice?" Carol put on a breathy, high-pitched voice and said, "PLEASE MISTER, PUT DOWN THAT GUN," bursting into laughter at her imitation of me. Even I had to laugh.

My grandmother, Mimi, called the next day. "Now sweetheart, your granddad and I are worried about you," she said. "You're not going to be carrying a gun, are you?" She was dead serious.

My family was sure there was no way I would get in, and I suppose I thought so too.

But a week later, a letter came from the department saying that I had been accepted into the 63rd recruit class. I was ordered to report to the Plans and Training division for prerecruit work until the class began.

Heart in my throat, I called Dalton. "I got in," I said.

"What?"

"I got into the department. Recruit school begins in October, and I've got a job in Plans and Training until then."

"What does that mean?" he asked.

"It's MPD's way of paying us until the training session begins. So we don't take another job."

"So, wait. You're really going to be a cop?"

"Yes, I am," I said. "I'm going to be a cop."

When he didn't say anything, I asked, "What do you think?"

"I guess this means you're not coming to Miami with me?"

"No," I said, surprised at my lack of hesitation. I had made my choice, and it wasn't him.

For once in my life, I hadn't sacrificed myself for a man.

2

The Maui Police Department bet money that I wouldn't make it through recruit school. Only about fifty percent of recruits end up graduating from the academy, and here I was, this thin *haole* girl with pipe-cleaner arms and a squeaky voice.

On our first day, as we sat in the department's huge lecture hall, Sergeant Kainoa told us that out of all the applicants—I assumed it was hundreds, but later understood it to be more like one hundred—ours were the only twenty-four applications accepted. There were so few of us compared to the size of the room. On the back wall, there was a photo of each recruit class, and I was surprised to see how small all the graduating classes were. We would only graduate eleven out of that original twenty-four.

I sat with my friend Kevin, who I met while we worked as prehires in Plans and Training. Kevin and I had become workout buddies, getting up at five every morning to go to the MPD gym before work.

That first day of recruit school, I felt proud. I was one of the elite. I was also a little distracted by thoughts of Dalton. Our relationship had already been strained by my joining the police force, and he was moving back to Miami in a matter of weeks. We were going to try the long-distance thing, and I had no idea how that would go.

Looking down at my notebook, I realized with horror that, like a high schooler, I had doodled his name in the margin. Some of the male recruits seemed to be checking me out, but I was thinking only of Dalton. I barely noticed them.

There had been one guy who caught my eye, an officer I met briefly in Plans and Training. This officer—Officer Davis, tall, handsome, Hawaiian, built—had come into Plans and Training with a smile that captivated me. We locked eyes and had an instant connection. *This is what love at first sight must feel like*, I thought briefly, dramatically, but realized I was just attracted to his good looks. I was still dating Dalton, so the moment passed and life went on. I hadn't seen him since then, but I remembered how he had made me feel.

Kainoa introduced us to our other instructors, who seemed cold. Cruel even. Reagan went over the schedule and told us when we would have an emergency vehicle operator course (EVOC), firearms training, arrest defense tactics (ADT), and physical training (PT). I felt a surge of excitement as he described all the maneuvers we would learn to do, but then he said, "I don't know why I'm bothering to go over this. Most of you won't even make it past the academics, and the rest of you will fail physical training."

I felt my muscles tighten when he said this. I had been around cops long enough in Plans and Training to know they liked to show up on the first day of class with badass attitudes. Still, I was intimidated. I was concerned about the PT and my lack of upper-body strength.

Next to me, Kevin nudged me and said, "Don't worry, Alli, you're a beast!"

I gave him a smile. We had been working out like crazy, running, lifting, and circuit training every single day. I was stronger than I looked. When the instructors looked at me, I was sure they under-estimated me. The odds were against me, but I knew something they didn't know—I had a determination like they'd never seen, and I couldn't wait to show them.

At break, they handed out granola bars, and we stood around awkwardly trying to meet each other. A chubby guy came up to me, chewing one granola bar and holding two more. "You're going out for the force?" he asked.

I nodded, wondering why else he thought I would be there.

"You don't look much like a cop," he said.

You don't either, Fatso, I wanted to say, surprised he had passed the weight requirement, but I held it in. It was our first day, and I was going to be spending nine solid months in training with him.

"You look like the most popular cheerleader in high school," Fatso continued.

"I wasn't a cheerleader," I said. "I was a soccer player, so watch your ass."

"Sorry," he said. "You just don't look like the cop type."

The next morning, I was so excited to start training that I was the first to arrive. Recruits aren't allowed to wear their uniforms outside the department, so I had to get dressed in the locker room prior to class. I loved putting on my gun belt for the first time. It was heavy and hurt my hip bones, but it gave me confidence I had never had before.

I sized up the other two female recruits in the locker room and concluded I might be able to hold my own against them. Penny Drinan had been in the military and was just like a man. A hard-ass. She would turn out to be our sergeant at arms, but she would struggle academically. Julia Loza was a pretty Filipina and more girlie, and she made a point of telling me that she had done some modeling in the past.

The men in recruit school were a mixed assortment, from meat-heads to nerds. I loved all the local boys—they were funny, humble, encouraging. But the white male recruits from the mainland were typical meatheads. Chauvinistic. Most were physically fit. Others were a little soft. The heavy guy from the day before was named Tom Pika. It turned out his father worked in the department, and I assumed that was why he was accepted. His connections made him arrogant even though he was far from qualified for the department.

I loved the training we did in recruit school—a long training in aikido, a great deal with the martial arts, lots of hand locks and learning how to control people you normally couldn't control. Sergeant Mankell taught us how to do hand-to-hand combat. We spent plenty of time getting hit and learning what it felt like to get hit without being stunned. My high school boyfriend, Josh, and I used to get into a lot of fights, some of them physical, but before joining the department, I had never been cracked in the face and I had never hit anyone in the face either. I came home one day and told Dalton we had practiced getting hit in the jaw all day and he just rolled his eyes. He was having a hard time watching his girl-friend become a cop.

During some parts of training, we had to keep a red band on our firearm hand. They taught us not to do anything with our firearm hand, because if you have something in that hand, how the hell are you going to draw a gun?

We also spent time on perspective training, training our eyes to look all around to avoid getting tunnel vision in a high-adrenaline situation.

"You'll need this for domestic violence calls," our instructor said. "You'll be fighting with the male to get him cuffed. Meanwhile, the female is coming at you with a frying pan."

My first day in ADT the instructor said, "Trust me, you're going to need to use everything I teach you in arrest defense tactics. You know why? Because criminals don't like to get arrested, and they'll do anything they can to get away from you." He looked around the room, appraising us. "Okay," he said. "We're going to start with some highly technical training. It's called 'Oh shit' training."

We all laughed, but he shook his head to indicate he was serious. "For example," he said, "what do you do if someone's on top of you pounding your face? That's an 'Oh shit' moment. A volunteer?"

Wanting to prove myself, I raised my hand.

He looked surprised but said, "Okay. What's your name?"

"ALLI?" I said. There were a couple of snickers. Even I could hear my cartoonish little voice.

"Okay, Alli, I want you to lie down on the ground."

I lay on the floor and he said, "Now, you have to do whatever you have to do to get me off of you." As he lowered his full weight onto my torso, everyone laughed. I honestly thought he would kill me. He was an enormous Hawaiian guy, two and a half times my weight. I couldn't breathe.

I didn't know what to do, so I bit him.

"Jesus Christ!" he said. He definitely got off me right away. Holding his arm in pain, he looked around quickly, trying not to look like a pussy. "You're a real alligator," he said. "Alli the Alligator." The nickname stuck, and the bite was hard enough to leave a permanent scar.

A few days later, a girl came up to me in the grocery store. I had no idea who she was, but she pointed at me and said, "You bit my boyfriend." At first she looked like she was going to bite *me*, but then she burst out laughing. So did I.

Usually ADT is the training that fails people in the academy. A lot of recruits can't hack it. The instructors exhaust you physically and mentally first, and then they make you fight for your life, just like you'll have to on the job. Some people have that crazy survival warrior instinct in them and some don't. It turned out that I did. Your body will either react or freeze, and the people who react become great cops. It isn't *thinking* that's going to save your life at moments like those.

Everyone teased me about taking the department so seriously, but I was passionate about being a cop. I was even elected president of the class. If a recruit did something wrong, I had to write a letter to the chief, explaining the situation and how I was going to stop it from occurring again. Julia would sandbag when we did physical training, and we would have to run farther as punishment. My friend Jonathan forgot his bulletproof vest one day, so I had to write a letter. I took on a lot of work, but I thrived on it. We had to be there by seven thirty in the morning, but I would get there at six to work out with Kevin before class started. When we finished at four thirty in the afternoon, I would stay until six to get the paperwork done. I never wanted to leave. For maybe the first time in my life, I felt like I was in the right place. By the time Dalton left for Miami I barely noticed his absence. I just stayed longer at work, energizing and exhausting myself.

At the end of my first full week without Dalton, Julia slammed her locker door and said, "How about a drink, Alligator?"

"I'd love to, but I'm tired. I need to go home and sleep."

"Oh come on, Alli. You never come out with us."

"I know," I said. "I'm sorry." But I wasn't really. I had avoided social situations, preferring work and Dalton instead. Plus, Loza was already making the mistakes most girls make coming into a department—sleeping with the patrol guys before recruit school even ended. I didn't want to associate myself with her. Cops want what they want, and they want women. It's easy for female cops to lose the respect of their beat partners and get labeled as sluts. I didn't want to do anything that would associate me with her.

"I just can't keep up," I complained to Loza on Monday morning. My shoulders ached, my legs ached, and even after spending the weekend recharging in bed, I had to drag myself in on Monday. We were doing high-speed car chases, training all day and into the night, and I was constantly tired. Loza was bouncing around like Tigger, swinging her long brown ponytail.

"I've got something that can help you," she said. She fished around in her bag and pulled out a little box. Popping open the top, she handed me a small red pill. "It's caffeine," she said. "Super-mega caffeine pill."

I looked at the pill suspiciously. "I'm not really much of a caffeine person," I said. "I don't even drink coffee. Just soda occasionally."

"Exactly why you need this," Loza said.

I swallowed the pill with my vitamin juice and we headed out to the course. All of a sudden I was wide awake. I could do K-turns and J-turns; I could run faster, run longer. The next morning I asked her if she had another one, and she gave me a small bottle with a few pills.

"Thanks," I said. "I'll pay you back. Where do you get them? GNC? The Vitamin Shoppe?"

"You can order them online," she said, and spelled out the name for me. "Phentermine."

A couple of days later, I went online to look for the stuff. Turns out it was actually an amphetamine, totally illegal to purchase in the US. You had to buy it from those sketchy Canadian websites where you purchase knockoff Viagra.

"You bitch," I said, shutting my laptop hard enough that it almost flew off the table.

I didn't know what to do. I was pissed at myself for being so naïve, and pissed at Loza, too. I stopped taking the pills immediately. Within hours, I started to feel lethargic. Tired. Hungry. Turns out I was having withdrawal symptoms. Phentermine is addictive.

"What the hell were you trying to do to?" I said to Loza in the locker room the next morning.

"What do you mean?"

"The phentermine," I said. "Amphetamines. Jesus Christ."

"What?" She acted surprised. "I didn't know."

"Bullshit. Why are you becoming a cop if you're not going to uphold the law? Is it because you like all the attention from the guys?"

"You're saying I joined the force for the guys?"

I turned away, disgusted. Everybody had labeled us best friends because we were the two pretty girls in recruit class, but I had never felt Julia was serious about being a cop. She was nonchalant about the rules. I was a by-the-book recruit, and she thought marijuana should be legalized. Plus, she was so damned flirty and used to be a model. Once she brought her modeling book to recruit class, which was weird to begin with, and then just happened to leave it in someone's patrol car so the whole department would see. I thought she was kind of shady, and I stopped returning her calls. Eventually, she dropped out of our recruit class, though she returned a year later and ultimately became a cop.

I started to worry that I wouldn't pass my drug test because of the phentermine. I had no idea how long it would stay in my system, and I spent a couple of really tense weeks that way.

My craving for the phentermine should have put me on alert. My family has a long history of addiction, mostly to alcohol. My mother, two uncles, and both maternal grandparents were alcoholics. High-functioning alcoholics, they liked to call themselves. Mimi, my grandmother, quit cold turkey when I was a child, and two years later my family did an intervention on my granddad. By now, they had both been sober more than twenty years. But my uncles were at the height of their alcoholism, my cousin was a heroin addict, and my mom, after enjoying fifteen years of sobriety during my childhood, had relapsed into alcoholism during her divorce. I know now that I had a predisposition toward addiction, but no one in my family ever talked about it that way. The rampant alcoholism was hardly a big secret; it was just something everyone laughed and joked about. No one in my family treated it seriously. No one thought it was a big deal.

I had smoked a lot of pot in high school with Josh but never tried anything else. I didn't even drink very much because I hated feeling out of control. I suppose you could say that phentermine was my first true addiction.

So when the drug test arrived, I was terrified. I knew if I tested positive, that would be it. I would be off the force. And I would murder Loza.

The day of the drug test, we lined up in the hallway while they inspected the bathrooms. It was easier and faster for the girls since there were only three of us. A female officer took us into the bathroom one by one. There was a special bluing chemical in the toilet to prevent me from diluting my urine with toilet water. The officer listened to me go, and I wasn't allowed to flush the toilet afterward. I handed her the cup and she tested the temperature right away and put a tape over the cup. Petrified, I initialed the cup, and thankfully, nothing showed up. I swore I wouldn't be so stupid in the future.

On graduation day, I received my badge. I wore, for the first time, my tailored uniform with my name embroidered on it, and white gloves. My Glock was signed over to me, along with three boxes of ammunition and a heavy, bulky radio. My mom came to graduation, of course, and so did my sister and brother-in-law and their baby girl, Maya. Predictably, there was no word from my father. My mom had emailed him in Florida to tell him I had started recruit school and again to tell him I was graduating. She asked him to at least send a card letting me know how proud he was of me. But there was no card. No call. He had wiped me clean from his life when I was nineteen.

Because I was the president of the class I got to make a big speech, and I won the notebook award, an academic award that made my mom proud.

As all of my teachers and instructors congratulated me, Sergeant Mankell handed me an envelope. "Here's the five bucks I owe you," he said. "I didn't forget."

I had no idea what he was talking about—probably some silly bet we had made—but when I opened the envelope later, I saw that in addition to a crisp five-dollar bill he had written a letter congratulating me. I will never forget what he wrote:

You have the heart of a lion, and you never quit.
You acknowledged your pain, but did not indulge it.
You are gentle and humble, yet sharp as a sword.
You remained generous in all that I have seen you do.
You are a warrior.

Only eleven of us had made it through to graduation. A bunch left after PT or ADT. Loza just didn't show up one day. One guy quit because of his wife, who couldn't tolerate the hours of recruit school. He was told that if his wife couldn't handle recruit school, she sure as hell couldn't handle him being on the job. Amazingly, Fatso graduated. The instructors beat him down constantly, but I guess because of his father he was passed.

As for me, I now belonged to the brotherhood. And I was finally doing something with my life.

3

There are different kinds of cops—investigators, who find facts, analyze, and problem-solve; detectives, who put together puzzles and solve mysteries; and basic cops, the guys who only wear the badge in order to kick people's asses. I was definitely an investigator. Fresh out of recruit school, I was itching to get into the community and find out what was going on.

I was also terrified. I was a *cop*. My responsibilities loomed large.

Luckily, I was going to spend four months riding around with field training officers before I had to go it alone. My first FTO, Agent Kane, reined me in. Kane was a tiny Asian man, soft-spoken, and a very talented officer. He taught me how to do everything by the book and how to be disciplined in learning about the law and managing my time.

"Alli," Kane said, "we're shorthanded on cops in Maui, so your time management is number one. You're not going to get home until midnight unless you learn to take care of your paperwork and evidence between traffic stops and calls."

Kane wasn't very confrontational, and I found myself getting into fights with beat partners while he wasn't watching over me. He did teach me how to sit and observe instead of getting myself into trouble every time I went on a case.

My second FTO, Al Torres, couldn't have been more different from Kane. He had a reputation for not exactly doing things by the book.

The first night I was out with Al, we spotted a teenaged kid riding his bike. We could tell by looking at him that he was a stoner, and we slowed down and drove beside him, watching him weave from side to side while he looked up at the sky. Al laughed and lit the kid up. The poor kid stopped, dropping his bike.

"What, man?" he asked. "I'm just trying to get home on my bike."

"Been smoking weed?" Al asked. "Been dealing?"

We could smell the weed on him, but the kid said, "Come on, man, don't take me in. I got nothing."

The kid had a pipe sticking out of the pocket of his pants, so Al said, "I'm seizing your pants!"

"You can't do that!" the kid said. He turned to me. "Can he do that?"

I nodded. "He can do that," I said, though I was pretty sure he couldn't.

"Pants!" Al said, holding out his hand, and the kid struggled to get his pants off without falling down. He handed them to Al and had to ride the bike home in his underwear. Later that night, his parents came to the station and filed a complaint.

A week later, Kevin and I were both riding with Al when we got a call from a store in the mall that a lady had stolen some jewelry. When we got there, the store detective was talking to her, and we could tell she was methed out. She was so thin she looked anorexic. She was barely wearing any clothes, just this little flowered dress and no underwear. When Kevin and I cuffed her, she went crazy, flopping around on the floor like a dying fish and trying to get out of her cuffs. Her little dress was riding up and you could see every-thing—it was a real mess. She fought us like crazy. Meth makes you strong, or at least makes you think you're strong. Al watched with amusement as we struggled with her. Finally, he took his giant boot and stepped on the woman's head.

He turned to me and let out a big laugh. "See, Moore," he said, "when you step on the freak's head, the freak stops moving."

For four months, I rode along with my field training officers, learning how to be a cop. After that, my sergeant put me in the Fishbowl while I awaited my first assignment. The Fishbowl, the receiving desk for Wailuku patrol, is where prisoners are booked and processed; most rookies spend a lot of time there. Instead of killing time watching TV with the receiving desk sergeant, I was studying the offender-based transactions, or OBTs—cop-talk for the arrest record. I wanted to find out who the major players and arrestees were on Maui during that time.

In the Fishbowl, I observed how different cops and receiving desk officers treated their detainees. I also learned how to build a rapport with the arrestees and the patrol officers. When I would take the detainees to their cells, I heard a lot of complaints about their treatment by arresting officers. I learned what officers were dicks and what officers were respected. There is a quote by Frank Barron—"Never take a person's dignity, it's worth everything to them and nothing to you." I felt everyone should be treated with respect, even those that broke the law. That is what I began to learn in the Fishbowl, and that lesson was hammered home to me when I hit the road again.

My life at this time revolved around work. I would get up at four a.m. to go to the fitness center, and then report to the Fishbowl for an eight-to-twelve-hour shift, studying arrest records and reading reports on Report Warrior, the template we used to record information about our cases. After that, it was back to the gym before going home to sleep for a few hours. I was in the best shape of my life, but my life had been funneled down to work and the gym. No hobbies. No beach. No social life. All my friendships from Lulu's had faded quickly once I became a cop, and my long-distance relationship with Dalton wasn't going so well.

I loved my life, but I was lonely.

Around this time, I ran into Officer Davis, the Hawaiian officer I had first seen in Plans and Training. He came into the Fishbowl with an arrestee, and I felt that connection again.

It turns out he did too.

He said, "You made it through the academy, huh?"

"Yes," I said.

"Congratulations. And I hear you'll be joining us in Bravo Watch."

Even I hadn't heard this yet.

"It will be great to have you," he said. "You look like you've been hitting the gym."

I turned red with embarrassment. "Thanks, Officer Davis," I said. I was planning to visit Dalton in Miami soon and had become obsessed with wowing him with my body.

"If we're going to be working together you have to call me by my first name," Officer Davis said.

"Okay, Charles," I said.

"Nah, my close friends call me by my Hawaiian name. Keawe."

"Okay," I said.

"Say it," he said, teasing me. "Ke-a-we."

"Okay," I said again. "Keawe." I knew he was flirting with me. I also knew he was married.

I had a few days off between leaving the Fishbowl and starting my first assignment, and I used them to visit Dalton in Miami. Seeing him when I got off the plane felt wonderful, but within minutes I could tell something wasn't right. He was gentlemanly, but he felt distant and cool, and I didn't fit in with any of his friends, who couldn't get past the idea that I was a cop. They were all deciding between getting law degrees or MBAs. On the last night of my visit, we went bowling, and his sister said to me, "You seem nice so I just thought I should tell you. He's cheating on you."

That was the end of our long-distance romance.

Back in Maui, my first assignment after the Fishbowl was Happy Valley. These are the largest projects on Maui and are mostly full of local Hawaiians, with a mix of Filipinos and a few white families. All poverty, all drugs. Ice—as methamphetamine is called in Hawaii—is an enormous problem in Maui, and Happy Valley is where the ice epidemic is hitting the hardest.

I was scared shitless working in Happy Valley. In MPD, you're solo—no one has partners—and if you're white, you stand out. Even more so if you're blond and a girl. I was a target for a lot of people because I was new, and they wanted to test me and see how far I would go.

Gangs from all over the island meet to fight in Happy Valley. If the Happy Valley Boys are going to beef with the Kihei Boys, or the Lahaina Boys are going to beef with the Wailuku Boys, they're going to do it in Happy Valley. When the cops are called, there's always the chance you'll be the first car there, so you have to react. You're not going to sit in a patrol car and wait for backup while potentially someone's getting hit in the head with a bat.

On my first felony traffic stop in Happy Valley, I was working Wailuku beat 10. An undercover officer called in and said, "Hey guys, I see this stolen car headed down Main Street."

I was so excited. I'd never done a felony traffic stop before, and I was just a minute away. When I got there I was alone. I identified the stolen car and lit it up. When the car pulled over, I got out of my patrol car and pointed my firearm at the car. A guy got out of the passenger side, pulling out these two giant pit bulls behind him.

"I'm letting them go," he said. "You watch it." The pit bulls snarled, straining at their leashes.

I started to shake, thinking I might have to shoot the guy, and if I did, he would let go of the dogs. I wasn't sure I could shoot both of them before they got to me. Meanwhile, the female on the driver's side was trying to toss her dope, the radio was blasting for me to update, and my firearm hand was shaking. I was behind the driver's side door and could hear the sirens, but at this point I was still solo.

"Put those dogs back in the car," a deep, confident voice ordered.

That voice was *mine*. I don't have that normal command presence that men or butch women have, but I do have this calm *man* voice that comes over me when I'm really nervous. I used that voice, and it startled the guy. I told him again to put the dogs away, and lo and behold, he did. I closed in on him, and when my beat partners finally showed up, we found a bunch of dope in the car and made the arrests.

I couldn't believe it—my first big awesome case. I was a cop.

I felt strong. Untouchable. Badass.

Until the next week.

One of my beat partners got into a high-speed pursuit on Honoapiilani Highway, and I joined in the pursuit. Abruptly, the guy we were pursuing turned his truck off the highway and onto a dirt road headed for the Maui Block. The Maui Block is an area of wilderness above Wailuku where most criminals hide out because it's treacherous and hard for us to navigate.

I was considered a pretty aggressive driver throughout recruit school and was keeping pace with the pursuit. The next thing I knew, I was looking at water. The nose of my patrol car was pointed down and I had to brace myself against the steering wheel to keep from falling into the windshield.

I was in some sort of Maui Block swamp, stuck in my car because of the angle—not to mention the water all around me. Thankfully the water was not very deep—it barely covered the engine block. I was going to radio in my predicament as soon as I felt the chase was over, but before I could do that, I saw some lights behind me and heard a bunch of laughter. My beat partners approached my car as I rolled down the window.

"Need some help, Alli?" one of them asked, and I thought the others were going to die laughing. I was on the verge of tears.

"Don't worry, honey. We'll get you out of there," one of the guys said condescendingly. Turns out they had caught the man we were chasing, and they made him use his own truck to tow me out of the ditch. For that they let him go. One of the guys took pictures, and they had lots of laughs, but they were decent about it. They never told any of the brass. It was the most embarrassing thing I had gotten myself into, but after a day or two I found it as funny as they did. Keawe kidded me about it in the station, and I was able to laugh with him. I guess it took badass me down a peg.

• • •

In Happy Valley, I earned the reputation of being a good cop. I wasn't arrest-happy like some of the others. If a guy was driving drunk and I knew he didn't have the money to bail himself out or pay the court for the DUI fine, I would make his wife come pick him up. When people living in that kind of poverty don't pay a traffic ticket because they can't spare seventy bucks, they get picked up and sent to jail. Then they can't work, and their families fall even further into poverty. I tried to keep that from happening.

We didn't have quotas when it came to writing traffic violations, but there was an unspoken (but sometimes spoken) requirement from our sergeants to issue traffic tickets regularly. In attempts to produce drug arrests stemming from traffic stops, I pulled people over all the time and learned all the traffic violations and even county codes, but I rarely, rarely wrote traffic tickets. I was often scolded by my sergeants for not issuing more traffic violations, but I felt that traffic citations were the wrong way to enforce the law. When people drove recklessly, I pulled them over, warned them, and enlightened them on how to drive. Why issue a hundred-dollar ticket to people in an economy where we all knew they probably wouldn't be able to pay?

Cops could be so insensitive when it came to issuing tickets. They just couldn't see the big picture. Often an officer would issue a standard hundred-dollar citation to someone who couldn't afford car insurance. If the woman is making minimum wage and has to choose between paying her traffic ticket or feeding her family, she won't pay the ticket. Then a warrant is issued for an arrest, and she is visited by a rookie patrolman at her home during dinner and arrested for contempt of court for failure to pay a traffic ticket. Of course, the asshole rookie cop doesn't take the time to figure out where her children could go while he takes her in because he's on a deadline and needs to get his arrest report done, so CPS is called and the children are removed from the home. The woman didn't have the money to pay the ticket, so why would she have the money to now bail herself out of jail? She's kept in county lockup until her arraignment, misses work—no call, no show—so she's fired. When she finally makes it to her arraignment, the judge scolds her, orders her to pay the court, and releases her. At that point, her children are in the custody of CPS and she no longer has a job, so CPS won't release the children to her. She can't find a new job because she has recently been arrested, and her life is officially effed up because of one traffic ticket.

That is not the reason I became a cop.

However, the second a guy hit or even threatened to hurt another person, he was going to jail. They always knew that about me in Happy Valley.

4

MPD covered three islands in Maui—Maui, Molokai, and Lanai—and it was the policy of the department to send rookies out to one of the smaller islands for patrol. After Happy Valley, the sergeant sent me to Lanai for a one-year assignment.

I wasn't thrilled about it. Lanai was a tiny little island, forty-five minutes by ferry from Maui, a backwater town with mostly dirt roads and not a single stoplight. It was a small community—three thousand people, predominantly Filipino, predominantly Catholic. I had no idea what I would do there.

My only consolation was that I was going to have a dog to take with me, a 180-pound gentle mastiff named Mo. My soon-to-be beat partner on Lanai, Walker, had agreed to take Mo from one of his church members. Mo's owner, a woman, had recently died, and her husband couldn't stand to keep Mo around because he was too much of a reminder of his wife. A dog breeder himself, Walker knew that Mo would do best with a female and asked me if I would take her. Without thinking, I said yes, though my landlord in Kihei freaked out until he saw how mellow and friendly Mo was. I had never had any dealings with mastiffs before and had no idea a dog could be so sensitive and loving. Mo became an important part of my life almost immediately.

My sergeants threw a going-away party for me before I left for Lanai, a huge barbecue at Sergeant Alvarez's house in Lahaina. Everyone came—my fellow recruits and all of my beat partners from Bravo Watch. I rarely drank alcohol, but I drank a couple of cans of Heineken that night—the chosen beer of most MPD officers.

Of course Keawe was there. With Dalton out of the picture, I had been fighting my attraction to him. Once we started working together, it was hard for either of us to deny that something was brewing between us, but Keawe was a married man.

I wore a long-sleeved gauzy shirt, and several times that night I caught Keawe watching me. At one point he came up and whispered in my ear, "Nice outfit, but it covers up too much of you." I found this very flattering, and that bothered me. Part of me was actually relieved that I was leaving because I was worried about what might happen between us if I stuck around.

I put off my departure until the last possible moment and had to leave straight from the party to catch the last ferry of the night to Lanai.

When it was time for me to go, Keawe walked me to my car, where Mo was quietly sleeping in the backseat. As I opened the door, Keawe said, "I don't know what I'm going to do without you, Alli." To my horror, he leaned in to kiss me. I quickly turned my head so he ended up kissing my cheek.

"Hey," I said. "What are you doing?"

"You know what I'm doing," he said.

"I also know that you have a wife," I said angrily.

I got into my car and slammed the door. As I drove away, I tried to brush off his behavior. He had been drinking and was being a dog, the way a lot of cops are dogs. But in the end, I was so pissed at him for threatening our friendship that once I got to Lanai I stopped taking his calls.

On Lanai, Mo became a station dog. He wasn't eating very well—Walker, thought he was in mourning for his old owner—so I wanted to keep him with me all the time. I didn't even ask my sergeant—I just brought him into work one day and everyone loved him. He started sleeping in the report-writing room and riding in my patrol car. He got the reputation for being a police dog, but he was never deputized. I found Mo to be a great tool for proactive police work. If I made a traffic stop, all he had to do was peek his head out the back window and the driver would cooperate. He rode on the ferry with me back and forth, and when people saw him coming, they just assumed he was a drug dog. There were always a few backpacks with dope in them left behind when Mo and I were on the ferry.

Although I wasn't thrilled about being in Lanai, it was there that I developed my real passion for being a cop. At first I thought it was a lazy town with nothing for me to do but surveillance on cockfights and dogfights. Before long, I recognized how many drugs there were on Lanai, coming and going. Ice had captured the community. It takes two hours to get from Maui to Lanai on a Jet Ski, less than an hour on the ferry, and there is no security whatsoever. Dealers were sending coolers with packets of ice on the ferry with grandmothers who looked like innocent picnickers. Often our informants would tell us that a shipment was coming over, but we could do nothing because the ferry was technically US Coast Guard jurisdiction. An informant's tip didn't give us probable cause to hold people on the ferry and stop them from entering Lanai before the Coast Guard got there. I was sure we had missed several opportunities to nail dealers this way.

My beat partner Walker and I began to figure out who the major players were on Lanai, and we stirred the pot by bringing the drug epidemic to light. We spent most of our time on Lanai trying to make a case against Pete Cordiello, one of the biggest drug dealers on the island. We made a lot of drug-related arrests. Because it was such a small place, we were always arresting someone's son, someone's husband, or someone's nephew, so of course there was retaliation from the community. On Lanai, you really live with the people you're working with. You'll arrest them for DUI on a Saturday night and see them at the grocery store on Tuesday morning.

Shortly after we initiated investigation into Cordiello, we were called to a party for noise disturbance. The party was at the community center in Lanai, but it had spilled out onto the lawn, and Walker and I found ourselves walking into a mob of people. It was dark, loud, and very crowded, but we were complacent about our approach—there was rarely trouble in Lanai. We asked around about the organizers of the party, but before we got any further, I saw Walker get tackled by three guys.

"Stop resisting!" I yelled. I lunged forward toward the guys while someone grabbed me from behind. I suppose they thought it would only take one guy to restrain the female cop, but they were wrong. I got my elbows into the guy so he would release me and then cuffed him quickly.

"Stop resisting!" I yelled again. "Stop resisting!" Two guys listened, but the last guy was still going at Walker. By this time people at the party were yelling at him to stop. One guy kept shouting, "Nuff! Nuff!" meaning *stop*. Everybody else was running. The guy was still fighting Walker hard, so I tased him and he fell to the ground.

Meanwhile, I was yelling "ten-fourteen" into my lapel mike—
officer down—and gave our location. The dispatcher could hear
us on the radio calling for help, but there was no one to help us.
Walker and I were the only two officers on duty.

"I'm having a heart attack!" the tased guy complained. "You're
killing me, bitch."

We arrested the tased guy and hauled him into the station. We
were pissed, but we were also scared. For a short period of time, I
thought I might not make it out alive.

The worst part was that my sergeant didn't press charges on
the guys who jumped us. He brought them into the station for a
talking-to and then let them go. Sergeant Ruben had been on Lanai
for eleven years, and it seemed to me he had learned to turn a blind
eye to what was going on.

After Walker and I got jumped at the party, I started to feel
afraid. I wanted to do my job, but I knew there would be repercus-
sions every time I did.

About a week later, I came home to find my apartment ran-
sacked. As soon as I opened the door I could see that everything
was all over the floor. Mo came running toward me—he acted like
a puppy when he was afraid—and I started to look around. Nothing
seemed to be gone, but every piece of furniture was turned over,
every drawer dumped out. What were they looking for?

I immediately called the station and told them what had happened.

"Now will you believe me?" I asked Ruben when I got him on
the phone. "They're targeting me. Someone's targeting me, and I'm
sure it's Cordiello or one of his goons."

I expected him to make light of it, like he usually did, but this
time he seemed to take me seriously.

"Tell you what, Alli," Ruben said. "I know you've got two bedrooms there. Usually we put two officers in the place, but we figured since you were a female you wanted your privacy." I listened to his condescending chauvinism. "Why don't we put a male officer in there with you so that you're not scared."

"I'm not *scared*," I said, furious, thinking, *Have you seen my dog?* "I just want to get this asshole into jail."

Nonetheless, Ruben put one of my beat partners, Steve, into the apartment with me. MPD owned these apartments and rotated officers through them. Most officers never stayed on Lanai more than their allotted time, but Steve liked it and stayed on Lanai, which was rare. He didn't want to go back and work on Maui because the others iced him out often. Even though he was an intelligent guy, some of the cops on Maui considered him a broke. He wasn't a ripper, but he worked hard and did very good job with his investigations. He just wasn't proactive. There were suspicions from the other guys that he was gay, and I suppose that's the real reason they iced him out.

Steve was a great guy and we got along very well. He liked to tease me about Mo. I had started cooking elaborate meals for Mo to entice him to eat—steak, potatoes, chicken—and Steve would come in and say, "Smells good. What's for dinner?"

"Sorry," I would answer. "This is for Mo. You're on your own."

I ended up feeling better having Steve there, though I wouldn't tell that to Ruben. I didn't want him to think I was some helpless female who needed a guy to protect her.

Ruben left me alone until a couple of weeks later, when he sent me out on a statutory rape case.

"I need a female to investigate this," he said. "You know, to be sensitive to this young girl. Her uncle came in and filed a report. Says his fifteen-year-old niece is giving consensual sex to her twenty-four-year-old boyfriend."

"Where are the parents?"

Ruben shook his head. "No father. Mom's an ice addict. This Uncle Max has custody. Seems like a good guy, loves her to death."

"Filipina?" I asked, and Ruben nodded. In the Filipino community, it's not that unusual for older men to date much younger girls, but in Hawaii it was illegal for anyone under sixteen to have sex with someone more than five years older. Ruben ordered me to take Lea's statement.

I headed out to the address he gave me, feeling uneasy. Sex crimes weren't really my thing. I was good with narcotics but didn't have a lot of training in sex cases, and none involving minors.

I didn't know it at the time, but from the very beginning, I shouldn't have been investigating this case. I had not been trained to deal with juvenile sex cases, which require special handling and a delicate investigative style. We had a sex crime unit that came from Maui to deal specifically with juveniles, but in this case, Ruben seemed to want to handle it directly. I felt uncomfortable taking charge of this investigation, but I had no choice. According to department policy, when the sergeant asks me to do something, I have to follow his orders.

A man in his thirties answered the door. "Come in, come in, I'm Uncle Max," he said. He was gracious and welcoming, especially under the circumstances. He had a beautiful, pearly smile, and so did the girl, Lea, who came to the door when her uncle called her.

"Hi, Lea," I said. "I'm Alli. I'm here to ask you a few questions."

Lea's eyes darted to Uncle Max. He patted her on the shoulder and said, "I'll leave you two to talk." It was clear her uncle adored her and wanted the best for her.

Lea seemed nervous, but I tried to put her at ease. "Don't worry," I told her. "You're not in trouble. You haven't done anything wrong. I just need to get some information from you."

We sat on the lanai outside, and I started asking questions about Chris, her boyfriend. "What's he like?" I asked. "Is he a special guy to you?"

She smiled that smile and ran her fingers through her hair. She had beautiful long Hawaiian hair. "Yes," she said. "He's my boo. He's a really great guy."

"Does he treat you well? Make you happy?"

"Yeah, he treats me so nice. No drugs, only weed. I couldn't live without him."

I asked her where she had met him and when, and she talked to me as if I was her girlfriend. She seemed to trust me and answered every single one of my questions. She was a lovely, sweet girl, Lea, a child in so many ways, and I was proud of how easy it was to make my case.

I got a full statement from Lea and ended up charging her boyfriend with more than twenty charges of sexual assault. She was very much in love with him, and when I arrested him she was devastated. A few days later he was able to make bond, and her uncle immediately filed a restraining order against him.

The next day Uncle Max called me. As soon as I heard his voice, I knew in my gut something was wrong.

He told me, "She's gone."

"Lea?"

"She's gone. No note, her phone's off, I can't reach her."

I drove out to see the boyfriend Chris's family, but they wouldn't cooperate. They kept telling me it was my fault.

Two days later, we found Lea and Chris in a field a half mile behind the Lanai police station, a rifle beside them. A double suicide. They left a long letter, very angry with the police department, very upset with their families for turning them in.

Their deaths rocked the community. Nothing like this had ever happened on Lanai.

I had sensed all along that there was something missing in the case, but I didn't have the experience to know exactly how it was supposed to go. Meanwhile, the Maui detectives started asking questions and began to investigate us for dereliction of duty. I didn't have the qualifications necessary to deal with a juvenile case, and I should never have been put on it. I got reprimanded, and I don't know what action, if any, was taken against Sergeant Ruben.

I couldn't help thinking that if the juvenile detectives had interviewed Lea, things might have gone very differently. Maybe she and Chris would still be alive.

Watching the devastation to Lea's family threw me back to my own high school years and to something I still held secret more than ten years later.

When I was fifteen, I had tried to kill myself too.

5

Suddenly I couldn't stand being in Lanai anymore.

I sat at the tiny kitchen table in the Lanai apartment, pretending to eat a bowl of cereal though I had no appetite, trying to decide what to do. I had two days off, and for the first time since joining the force, I was thinking of taking them. Normally I would spend the day catching up on reports and trying to work on my case against Cordiello. Today I had no appetite for work. Since Steve was working all weekend, Mo and I were alone.

I felt shaken and physically ill when I thought about what had happened to Lea. I had had tunnel vision; I just wanted the confession so I could make the arrest. I had forgotten this was someone's life. Now, that life was over, and I felt guilty for any part I may have played in that.

I couldn't get Lea out of my mind, and sitting in the station five hundred yards from where we found her body wasn't going to help the situation.

Lea. Her incandescent smile. The innocent, trusting way she told me everything about her boyfriend, as if I were her older sister, her best friend. Someone on her side, when she hadn't had many people on her side in her life.

She was a kid! Just turned fifteen. She couldn't possibly have known what she was doing. Ending her life, devastating her family.

I got up from the table and poured my untouched cereal into the garbage.

I had once been that kid, a kid in a relationship that wasn't good for me. A kid intent on killing herself, and I had almost succeeded.

It had happened more then ten years before, when I was a freshman in high school, fourteen years old, locked in a way too intense relationship with Josh.

Shortly after I turned fifteen, I got pregnant. I didn't want to think about it for even a minute, so as soon as we could, Josh and I went to get an abortion. Our only choice was a Planned Parenthood office with picketers outside. *Baby killer*, an old lady yelled at me. Couldn't she see I was practically a baby myself?

My mom was the most caring, supportive mother in the world, but I was too ashamed to tell her about the abortion. I could have told my sister, who was in college. They would have helped me and come with me, but I felt if I didn't tell them, it wasn't really happening. I never told anyone but Josh.

Afterward, my life felt like a complete wreck. There was the abortion, all my guilt, and the exhaustion of keeping it secret. There was Josh, who was controlling and abusive. There was my father, living somewhere in town with his secretary but refusing to give us his address. My mother, back on the bottle as her method of coping. And my sister away at college, happy to be away from our mess of a family. I had even lost soccer—kicked off the team because of my shit grades.

I had nothing left, and all I wanted to do was die.

I sneaked out in my mom's minivan one night, but instead of meeting Josh like I usually did, I drove all over the city—past Josh's house, past the high school, past my grandparents' house. I knew exactly what I was doing: I was saying good-bye to my life.

I headed to Tijeras Canyon, not far from where my uncle lived. I found the perfect cliff. Getting the speed up to ninety miles per hour, I unclipped my seat belt and took my eyes off the odometer. I felt relaxed and ready as I watched the cliff approach. I kept my foot on the gas, and the last thing I remembered was the side of the mountain.

I woke up in a helicopter. With fractured ribs and a ruptured spleen, blood oozing down my face from a head wound, I was disappointed that I was still alive. It turned out that taking off my seat belt had saved my life. If I had been wearing it, the engine that ended up in the front seat would have crushed me.

"Were you trying to kill yourself?" a voice asked. I couldn't even see who was asking the question. Still, my lie was automatic.

It was an accident, I was just driving too fast.

The Albuquerque police suspected a suicide attempt. There were no skid marks on the road, no evidence that I had tried to stop or swerve. I continued to lie. When I told my parents it was an accident, they believed me. My father did, anyway, but my mother suspected the truth. She never said so, but I could tell by her actions—moving me to a different high school, working with Josh's parents to break us up—that she was trying to fix the situation without actually talking about it.

In order to keep up with my lie, I pretended I felt lucky to be alive. I actually started to do well in school, and subsequently my life began to improve. Instead of dealing with the feelings that had led me to that cliff, I lied away their very existence.

To this day, I had told no one the truth about that suicide attempt. Or the pregnancy that preceded it.

It was easy now to blame it all on teenage drama, family angst, but what I felt then was real. That hopelessness, that despair—what would have happened if I had succeeded that night? What would my mother, sister, and grandparents have done if they had lost me?

These questions made me shaky. Normally I was tough. Guys on the force would be crying their eyes out over a body we found or some brutal domestic case, and I would be calm as could be. Cold, even. But Lea was stirring up a part of me even my coldness couldn't cover.

I wondered: somewhere deep inside me, was I still that girl? I carried a firearm now and made arrests, but had I really changed? I had thought that throwing myself into work would make my life complete, but suddenly I felt as lonely and scared as I had felt that day in Tijeras Canyon.

I needed to go for a run to clear my head. I threw on a T-shirt and some running shorts and was starting to do leg stretches when my phone beeped.

Keawe.

Beep, beep.

Keawe again.

I had done nothing but ignore his calls for months, but today without even thinking I picked up the phone.

"Hey," I said.

"So you're finally talking to me again," he said. I could almost hear him smiling. No sarcasm at all in his voice.

"Maybe," I said lightly. "Today, anyway."

"I'll take what I can get," he said.

I put the phone on speaker and continued to stretch, pushing away Mo, who was getting excited about a run. A small slice of light from the window cut across the room.

"I heard about your case," Keawe was saying. "The girl. I'm sorry."

"It was horrible," I said. "She was barely fifteen years old."

"It's not your fault, Alli," Keawe said. "You were doing your job. The chief said you're proving yourself as a ripper."

"A lot of good that's doing me," I said. "I did exactly what Ruben told me to do, but it wasn't right. We weren't following procedure. There's going to be an investigation." My voice cracked on that last word, and I was embarrassed.

"If there's an investigation," Keawe said, "Ruben will get the rap for it. Broke-ass."

I sat on the floor and drew my knees to my chin. "I don't care about that," I said. "I just care that there are two people dead because of me." Secretly, though, I was pleased at Keawe's compliment. Since joining the department I'd been working my ass off, putting in insane overtime, taking the senior officers' cases, keeping myself in top physical shape so I could fight if I had to, all the while learning how to defuse situations to make fighting the last resort. At MPD, you were either a ripper—a hardworking go-getter everyone could count on—or a broke. Ruben was a broke: a lazy, unreliable oaf who could make a volatile situation worse.

"Those kids aren't dead because of you, babe," Keawe was saying. "No one said this line of work was full of happy endings. We should talk about it more. What are you doing today?"

"Working?" I said.

"Bullshit. You've got the day off."

"How do you know?"

"I've got good investigation skills too," he said. "I've also got some time. Why don't I take the ferry to Lanai and we can hang out?"

"What about your family?" I asked.

"Oh, they're in California for a few days," he said casually. "Visiting Colleen's parents."

His plan was so transparent. His wife and children out of the picture for a while, he was ready to swoop in on me, just as he had tried to do the night before I left Maui. But he had been calling me at least twice a week since I got to Lanai. All those times couldn't have been predatory. Some of them must have been in honor of the friendship we had started to build while we worked together.

"So what do you say?" he asked, trying to sound casual. Then, with more feeling, he said, "I've really missed you, Alli."

"Don't come to Lanai," I said. "I've got to get off this island. I'll come to Maui."

"You will?"

I found myself smiling at how excited he sounded. "Yes," I answered. "I'll take the ten-thirty boat. I'll call you when I get in."

"No need to call," he said. "I'll meet the ferry."

I had exactly forty-five minutes on the ferry to wonder why the fuck I was agreeing to see Keawe, but in typical fashion I avoided thinking at all. Instead, I watched a group of dolphins off to the right, one of them doing triple axial spins. Molokai passed off to the left. I nodded at one or two people I knew on the ferry, but most people on board were tourists. Three twenty-something girls with great bodies and bad sunburns. A honeymoon couple. A golfer who looked pretty dejected. It was late July, high tourist season.

The ticket taker came around, chatting to everybody. The golfer handed him money and the ticket taker shook his head. "You got to buy the tickets before you get on the boat," he said.

"What do you do with stowaways?" the golfer asked.

"They get to go halfway for free."

The golfer laughed.

The ticket taker said, "You can pay on the other end."

The ferry was expensive for tourists, but they offered *kama'aina* rates for Hawaiian residents, and MPD always paid for my ferry trips. That was part of my compensation.

I liked listening to everyone's conversations but couldn't bring myself to start up a conversation on my own. No one talked to me, either. Maybe it was because of Mo. He loved riding the ferry back and forth, but people usually kept their distance from a 180-pound mastiff. My mom or sister would have made best friends by the time we got to the other side. They were so different from me.

When we docked in Lahaina, I spotted Keawe immediately. He was leaning against the fence, wearing a powder-blue T-shirt that cut just at the place on the biceps a girl loves to look at. He smiled and walked toward me for a hug.

"Hi, gorgeous," he said. The hug felt tense, not because of me, but because of those around us. Maui was so small—someone was bound to know at least one of us. It had to be a friendship hug, in case someone saw. The hug was just long enough for me to feel the heat of his skin. I looked up at his face—his smooth brown skin, his close-cut black hair, his warm brown eyes. *He* was the gorgeous one.

"So where do you want to go?" he asked. He patted Mo on the head. "The beach? Should we dump the mutt and get some lunch?"

"Sure," I said. It didn't matter what I said at this point because we both knew where we were going.

My shakiness disappeared once I was with Keawe. Within moments, I felt strong again, no longer vulnerable to the tragic mistakes of teenage girls. He felt like my savior.

Unfortunately, my good sense was gone too.

In less than half an hour, we were in my apartment in Kihei, pulling each other's clothes off.

We spent a day and a half holed up in my apartment. Keawe went out to L&L for chicken katsu once or twice, but mostly we stayed in bed.

And we talked. I told him about Pete Cordiello and how frustrating it was to not be able to bring him down. We talked about Lea. I cried a little over that, and at one point I told him, "I don't think I'm tough enough to be a cop."

"I don't believe that for a second, Alli," he said. "You've held your own. Look at you, coming into the department a *haole* girl and turning out to be president of your recruit class. You know what kind of bets we placed on you?"

"Yeah, I heard." MPD cops were huge sexists, but they did respect female cops once they proved themselves. I knew I had earned respect within the department, but the outside community was a different story. Every time I arrested someone, it was "You *haole* bitch!" Trying to gain the trust of someone who hated me the second they saw me had given me some verbal judo skills, but it sure as hell wasn't easy.

We didn't talk about his wife. He never brought her up and neither did I. When she called, he politely took the phone onto the lanai. They were short conversations, exchanges of information. Married conversations. Keawe and Colleen had been married for seven years. He told me there wasn't a whole lot left between them except their three beautiful little children.

This weekend with Keawe was just what I needed. He was attentive and sweet, and he had the most incredible way of making me feel loved with just a look. The sex was phenomenal. But I knew it had to stay a onetime thing; there was no way in hell I was getting deeply involved with a married man. The next day, I would go back to Lanai, he would pick his wife up from the airport, and that would be that.

"I'll call you tonight," he said when he dropped Mo and me off at the ferry. I tried not to roll my eyes.

"I'll be waiting," I said, laughing. I was sure he had gotten what he wanted, and maybe I had too. I didn't want to dwell on any feelings I might be having about him.

But he did call that night. He called just after eleven, and we talked until three in the morning. Talked about anything. Every little stupid thing that popped into our heads. His pajamas had a hole in them. I needed to get a new toaster. He loved jelly doughnuts. Mo had bad breath. He hoped his softball team would win the next day. All these things were so inconsequential, but I hadn't had anyone to talk to like that since Dalton and I had broken up. I had never been very good at having lots of girlfriends to giggle and share things with, but I had almost always had a boyfriend. I missed having one now.

We laughed a lot, quietly—his wife, still on California time, was sleeping, and he was speaking to me from the bathroom at the other end of the house.

The next day I felt energized, more like myself again, and I threw myself straight back into work.

6

"You seem better, Alli," Walker said when I walked into the station on Monday.

"I am better," I said, and the two of us went straight back to dealing with our buddy Cordiello.

It killed me that we hadn't been able to pin anything on Cordiello yet. We had finally intercepted one of his packages, but he sent a runner to pick it up, making it impossible for us to connect the dope to him. Walker and I could never figure out what he did to scare people, but Cordiello was widely feared. It was hard to get anyone on Lanai to speak out against Pete Cordiello. He was smart enough to build a family and a lifestyle. He wasn't a troublemaker, and he didn't hang out with troublemakers. He was always respectful with police officers. Yet we knew by the numbers of Jet Skis and ATVs he was buying, by the elaborate parties he gave—flying strippers in from Oahu and paying for all the beer—that he was a major player.

Eventually we would catch him, I knew that. These guys weren't smart enough to not get caught. We *do* catch them, and then they leave the women and children who love them with the house that gets seized and the vehicles that get seized, and that's a whole other mess. But for now, his neighbors weren't talking, and our surveillance hadn't panned out yet.

Lieutenant Ruben, still dealing with the MPD chief over the Lea case, saw Walker and me plotting, and specifically said, "Don't stir up trouble, you two. We need to keep our profile low and exemplary for the next few weeks."

We didn't listen. Desperate to find out where Pete stored his dope, we talked Ruben into letting us do random boat checks. Technically MPD had no jurisdiction on boats, but Ruben okayed it as a proactive measure and told us not to get into trouble.

We decided to do a boat check that night. Boats were where fifty percent of our dope came from, and I was sure if we did enough of them we'd locate Pete's.

At the docks, we saw some Matson shipping containers that were of interest to us.

"What do you think?" I asked Walker.

"Let's go for it," he said.

We chose one to inspect but struggled to get it open.

"Let's try another one," Walker said.

"Nah," I said. "This one may be extra secure for a reason." We used all the force we could produce between the two of us and got it open.

"Shit!" I yelled.

"Literally!" Walker said.

The container was full of manure, now pouring out onto us.

"Ruben is going to kill us," I said. We had to go into the office tracking manure into the station. We left manure in the brand-new patrol car.

Keawe loved that story when I told him about it on the phone that night. We talked for two hours, and another two hours the next night.

What the hell was I doing?

I had never wanted to be messing around with anyone I worked with. Sure, I had gotten hit on left and right in the department. All the female recruits get hit on. But at the beginning of recruit school, Sergeant Kainoa sat me down and told me, "The best way to get through this is to do it without a guy." He was basically telling me not to sleep around like so many of the girls did. I had consciously avoided being labeled a slut all this time, and now I had slept with Keawe.

I didn't see him for another three weeks, but we talked almost every day, and I found myself thinking about him way too much. As my days on Lanai wound to a close, I started to get nervous. There would be no way to avoid Keawe once I was back on Maui full-time. MPD was such a small department, more like a family than an employer. It had its politics and bad apples, but the people that made up the department were like no other. Keawe and I were part of the same family—we were going to see each other all the time.

Shortly before I left Lanai for good, I was heading out the door to the station one day and called to Mo as usual. He didn't come. I found him on the couch asleep and tried to awaken him.

"Mo," I said. "Come on, boy." It took me half an hour to coax him into my car. There was no way I could pick him up, so he had to get in on his own. He seemed to be in incredible pain, and I drove him immediately to the vet.

"He has cancer," the vet told me after running some tests. "It's late stage. Has he been sick for a while?"

"I've had him less than a year," I said. "I don't know. I was told he was in mourning for his previous owner, and that was why he wasn't eating."

She nodded. "I think he's been sick all this time," she said, and then repeated, "It's very late stage."

"How late?"

I didn't need to hear the answer. We had to put Mo down that day.

Mo had become important to me in such a short time, and I was devastated. I called my mom in tears and she spent a long time consoling me. Then I called Keawe.

"I'm really sorry," he said. "I wish I was there to hold you. But in a week, you'll be here, and I'll be able to help."

I stayed home from work the day Mo died, and the next day Sergeant Ruben called me into his office.

"I want you to put the Lea case out of your mind," he said. "Start with a clean slate back in Maui. These things happen and they aren't pretty, but we have to do our jobs."

Lea was the last thing I wanted to talk about with him. I changed the subject.

"I'm just pissed I'm leaving you with Cordiello," I told him.

"You can't make it personal," Ruben said. "There's always another dirtbag following in his footsteps."

Ruben was good at turning a blind eye to the ice that was coming and going on Lanai, but he was right about Cordiello. I was smart enough to know that catching one dealer wasn't going to end the ice epidemic. After my year on Lanai, I was ready to move to a new town, a bigger town, and find out who the players were.

• • •

"Woo hoo, we're getting the narcotics girl," Officer Keanu said when I walked into the Lahaina station my first day back. He was grinning ear to ear, probably already planning to throw his work in my direction. Keanu was a bit lazy, never following up, never doing his paperwork. A broke, and everybody knew it. It was funny, but things at MPD operated outside of racial stereotypes. The islands were such a melting pot of Asians, Polynesians, haoles, that you almost never ran into issues of race at MPD. It all boiled down to work ethic. Ripper or broke.

"Officer Moore. Welcome back to civilization."

Keawe's voice. I froze. I hadn't expected to see him so soon.

I forced myself to turn around. With Keanu's eyes on me, I felt I was facing a test.

"Thank you," I said, as casually as possible. "Surprised to see you here. I thought you worked Wailuku."

"Do," he said, "but something brought me to Lahaina this morning."

"Damn you," I said later, when he showed up at my apartment. "You could have given me some warning. No one can know anything happened between us, you understand? *No one.*"

"I know that," he said, handing me a bouquet of flowers. "I'm sorry. I couldn't resist. These are for you."

I took the flowers and smelled them. He stepped into my apartment and closed the door.

"Is this how it's going to be now?" I asked him.

"Yes," he said, before he kissed me. "This is how it's going to be."

Keawe: my best friend, and now my lover.

At first, it was perfect. We spent a lot of time working together during the day, and he would always let me know if he was coming over that night. I put in four or five hours of overtime each day, so I normally didn't get home until ten o'clock. If he was free, we had a couple of awesome hours together. In the morning, I would go to work again without worrying about someone at home whining because I didn't pay enough attention to him. For a workaholic, the arrangement was ideal.

We were obsessed with each other. Whenever he left my apartment to go home, he would call me the minute he got into his car and talk to me all the way home, until the garage door went up at his house. I loved every single thing about him—the boyish dimples at the sides of his mouth, the way his smooth forehead creased when he wanted to say the right thing, his tendency to start singing "Moloka'i Slide" and other Hawaiiana at the oddest moments. He told me he loved me almost right from the start.

Keawe also taught me a lot about work in those early months— how to talk myself out of a situation instead of fighting my way out, how to listen to people first before reacting. He was so steady, so reassuring. Keawe embodied everything I loved about Hawaiian men. He was strong, intelligent, so compassionate, a family man, a good dad, close to his parents. Solid, and not a heavy drinker, which was rare for a Hawaiian cop.

I only dreaded the weekends, which for Keawe meant "family time," and for me meant forty-eight hours without him. I started to work more and more on the weekends so that even the chief was telling me to go home. I either wanted to be at work or with Keawe. Those were the only two ways I wanted to spend my time.

Late one Saturday afternoon on an extra shift, I was working a UEMV (unauthorized entry of a motor vehicle) case on Hanakao'o Beach on the edge of Lahaina. A tourist's car had been burgled and I was just wrapping up, checking the car for fingerprints, when an SUV pulled into the parking lot and parked next to us.

Keawe's SUV.

He got out of the car with his family and walked over to me casually. "Hi, Alli," he said. "What case you working?"

Behind him I could see his wife with their children. I was seeing Keawe's kids for the first time. They were so tiny! They wore adorable swimsuits and carried their beach gear, laughing and giggling, excited to be coming to the beach.

Why are you talking to me? I wanted to say to Keawe. *I hate you.*

His wife, Colleen, came over to say hello too. She was tall, very thin and pretty, with long straight brown hair. She held the little girl in her arms as she reached out to shake my hand while Keawe introduced us.

"Sorry," she said, "I've got to get Sacha into her swim diaper." She carried the girl back to the car.

A *diaper*. This is a baby, I realized.

I watched Keawe's family as they walked away from me and headed across the street to the beach. I wrapped up my case quickly and got back into my patrol car, where shame dropped like a curtain around me. I fought tears as I struggled to put the key in the ignition.

I wanted the affair to end. How could I do what I was doing to such a wonderful family? Three little children. One of them a baby. I was doing exactly what my dad had done.

When I got home, I wrote Keawe a long breakup letter and left it in his locker at work the next morning. He did not say anything to me about the letter, and I did my best to avoid him, but a couple of days later when I was driving home from work, he lit me up in his patrol car. Pulled me over.

"What the fuck are you doing?" I asked him. "Jesus!"

He handed me back the letter I had written. "I'm not ready to get this," he said.

"Keawe, I can't be that woman. I can't do this to your family."

He cut me off. "We'll work it out," he said. "We'll work it out. We'll be together, I promise."

I didn't really believe him. Something had changed for me that day on the beach. Before, I had thought of his family as separate from our relationship, as an extra in his life; I had fooled myself into thinking that *I* was his life. But he had a life—*I* was the extra.

In the four months since I had returned to Maui, I had wondered who would be my Pete Cordiello here, that guy I couldn't pin down, that guy I pursued in some sort of crazy quest. Now I understood that it wouldn't be a criminal this time, a small-time narcotics dealer or big-time drug trafficker. It would be a gorgeous Hawaiian man with a family he loved and a mistress he was obsessed with, and no reason at all to arrange his life any differently.

7

In Hawaii, the most prestigious private schools are the Kamehameha Schools. Founded in 1887 by one of the last descendants of King Kamehameha, they have a nine-billion-dollar endowment and are among the richest private schools in the country. Tuition is modest, so families don't have to be rich to go there, but you can only get in if you're Hawaiian. You actually have to prove your ancestry when you apply for admission. The schools promote Hawaiian values, and every Hawaiian wants his kids to go there. Keawe was no exception. The Kamehameha Schools, he told me, were the reason he couldn't leave his wife.

"The boys are three," he explained to me one night. "They'll be old enough to apply in a year, and Sacha the year after. We just have to wait until they're in, babe, and then we can be together. If they come from a divorced home, more than likely they're not going to get in."

He had been especially attentive since the day at Hanakao'o Beach. He didn't want to lose me—I got that—but he couldn't make a commitment either, and I refused to wait for some god-damned school admissions process to determine the outcome of our affair.

"I can't wait that long," I said. "It's . . . horrible. It's . . ."

"I know," he said, caressing my neck. "You know I want to be with you."

"But I picture you with her all the time. How do you, how can you—?" Of course I was talking about sex. I couldn't bear to think of him cheating on me with his wife.

"There's nothing left between us," Keawe said. "She's a great person and a really good mom, but I'm just not in love with her anymore. We've been married for seven years. It happens."

I wanted to believe him, of course, but I hated more than anything the idea of being the other woman. Like my dad's slutty secretary. I didn't want to be that person. God, how I didn't want to be that person.

I would never have asked Keawe to leave his wife for me. I was the product of divorce, and I couldn't bear the thought of doing that to someone else's children. We made an agreement that once the kids got into Kamehameha, he would ask Colleen for a separation.

I longed to be with him now. I wanted to be able to go out to dinner with him, or go to the movies. I wanted to hold his hand while we walked down the street. I wanted a real boyfriend. I didn't want to spend all of our time together in my apartment with the drapes closed, lying to everyone.

But that's exactly how it was.

• • •

It had been eight months since I started my affair with Keawe, and still no one knew about it. Around this time, I learned that another female cop, Dina Johnson, was having an affair with my old recruit school instructor, Sergeant Mankell. I barely knew Dina—she was on Alpha Watch and I was on Bravo—but sometimes we passed each other in the locker room and chatted. She was big on inviting me out to the bars, but I never went. She was my age, African-American, very pretty. Originally from Chicago, she had moved to Maui with her family fresh out of high school and was as in love with the island as I was. We had that in common.

When I found out Dina was having an affair with Ed Mankell, I thought back to the wonderful letter he had written me when I graduated from recruit school, and it made me a little sad. A little disappointed in Sergeant Mankell. He had young children too, just like Keawe.

Dina kept pushing a friendship, so one day I took her up on her offer to go out for drinks. I never did anything but work or hang out with Keawe, and it felt strange to sit in a bar with a girl my age. *A girl in her twenties should have lots of friends*, I thought.

Dina liked to drink, and I watched her slam down a couple of beers while I had a soda. This was exactly why I didn't like to socialize with other cops.

"You know about me and Ed?" she asked, after beer number three.

"I heard."

"It sucks," she said. "I'm an idiot, I know. It's just—"

"Me too," I said.

"What? You? The perfect Officer Moore?"

"Not so perfect," I said.

"Who is it?" she asked.

I took a deep breath. I wanted someone to know. "Keawe," I said.

She nodded. "I can see it."

"I hate it," I said.

"I know. You love him, but you hate it."

It made me feel slightly better to have shared this with Dina. I made her promise not to tell a soul, but later Keawe found out that she had told Mankell.

So much for making a girlfriend.

To avoid thinking about Keawe, I threw myself into work. Now that I was back in Maui, there were bigger players, bigger cases. Even though I was still on patrol, I started to build up a base of confidential informants, CIs. I wasn't technically supposed to be doing that yet, but I found it really useful in my narcotics work. I was gradually discovering that operating by the book wasn't always the best strategy for me.

I found that building a strong CI base and keeping my CIs in line was a hard job. Every cop has a different technique. Some like to threaten people into being informants. For others, it's all money-based. My thing was talking, building a rapport. If I worked a domestic abuse case, I would say, "What's up with your husband? Why is he trying to fight us when we're trying to arrest him? This isn't just alcohol behavior. Is he smoking crack?" I would flat out ask if he was an addict, and to my surprise, a lot of the women would say, "Yes, yes, he is on drugs." Then I could say to the guy after we arrested him, "Look, this is a problem. Now I know you're smoking crack and I'm watching you. But you can help me out. Who are you getting your dope from?" Over time, as trust built up, they would lead me to their small-time dealers, who then led me to the major traffickers.

I treated my CIs as friends, and they told me things that were happening in the drug world, things cops usually wouldn't know. I found out whose girlfriend was sleeping with someone's dealer, and I would target the girlfriend and say, "I know you're sleeping around on this guy to get dope, so why don't you work for me instead? That way you're protected. You still get your dope, and I get my target."

Some of my CIs were addicts, and others were just people in the community that were scared and fed up with the drug dealers. It's amazing the kind of people you meet in the drug world. I had one CI from Lahaina, a female, a solid CI. Sharon Benzos was a well-known real estate agent in Maui, forty-five years old, three kids, beautiful home in Keokea, drove a BMW—no one would ever pinpoint her as a meth user. She became a CI because I had arrested her for possession, and she was terrified of going to jail, terrified that her husband was going to find out. When I offered her the CI option, she took it. She understood that ice was bad for the community. She wanted to stop using, but she couldn't; rehab wasn't an option for her because then her family would find out. Because she was a user, I had problems keeping her in line. She tended to be erratic, and her information wasn't right on. But I took care of her, and I paid her well.

I always paid my CIs well. If they were going to make a buy for me from a target I was interested in, I would pay them at least a hundred bucks. Sometimes two hundred if the department would allow it. When you're working with addicts, the law says they can't use. They sign papers when they start working as CIs. We take their photos, and they have numbers that go into the search warrants to protect their identities, but they couldn't use, and they couldn't get arrested. The thing is, how are they going to make buys for you if they're not using? So I always made sure I gave them enough money to keep them in the drug world using. I would be really open with them and say, "Dude, are you using? If so, just tell me. Let's hit a target that you're not buying from, and if you want help, we'll figure out how to get you into rehab afterward."

When I was on patrol, I was really vocal about how passionate I was about narcotics work. I got the message through to my captains that I was a great patrolman but I could also do drug work at the same time.

One day my sergeant, Sergeant Wilkes, came up to me and said, "How would you like to do a little work with vice, Moore?"

"I would love it, sir!" I said. Vice was my dream.

"Patrick needs someone for undercover," he said, "and I'll be honest with you. He hasn't had an easy time getting female officers to do this in the past. But if you're game . . ."

"Tell him I'll do it," I said impulsively, knowing full well what he was asking me to do. They needed someone to go undercover as a prostitute, and none of the other girls would do it. I was so dedicated to the job that I didn't care.

Prostitution was not a huge problem in Maui—generally MPD only arrested one or two prostitutes in a year, and sometimes none at all. But the chief wanted to do a reverse sting and get the johns in order to send the message that prostitution would no longer be tolerated.

There was a prostitute lane in Happy Valley where guys knew they could go and pick up. Our first undercover operation went down there early in the spring. My job was to wear Daisy Dukes and high heels and get johns to offer me dope or money for sex.

We got nine guys that weekend. I wasn't the one who arrested the johns. There was an arrest team, so I never felt unsafe. Officers were on the roof, looking down on me to make sure I didn't get pulled into a car or anything.

The undercover was so successful we did a second sting the next weekend, this time in Lahaina. We got three johns, but more than that we sent a message to the community.

MPD videoed the whole operation to use for training purposes, and it wasn't long before Keawe saw it.

He was furious.

"I don't want you doing that again," he said. We were at work, sitting in his patrol car, pretending to talk about a case.

I just laughed. "It's my job." I said. "And you're not my boss."

"None of the other girls do it. You just have to say no. They can't make you."

"It's really successful," I said. "It works."

"I don't want my girlfriend dressing up like a whore."

When I didn't say anything, he said, "Don't you know the vice guys are watching this video of you all miked up and videoed up? Dressed like a slut. You have any idea what kind of comments they're making about you?"

"I can guess," I said. "Guys are going to do that."

"It's fucking embarrassing hearing them talk about my girlfriend like that."

"Except they don't *know* I'm your girlfriend."

"I just want you to stop."

"How can you ask me that?" I said tersely.

Keawe frowned. "You have to understand, this is not a good situation for me."

"And this is a good situation for *me*?" I said. "You're an asshole. You have a wife, a family, and expect me to act like your girlfriend in private and nothing in public?"

"Hey, you knew what you were getting into, Alli. We just need a little time and—"

"Time? I'll give you time," I said, opening the car door. "Here's your time, fucker!" I slammed the door and stormed off. I don't know if he would have followed me or not, but the sergeant walked up and I had to fall into step with him.

"You still here, Moore?" he asked.

"Yeah, I've got a lot of work to do."

Work was the only way I was going to get by without Keawe, I decided. I needed to move on, forget about him.

I hated that Keawe was interfering with my work, which was the thing I most loved about my life.

He called later that night, and then came over. Of course we got back together.

I tried to break up with him a couple of times after that, but it never lasted. We were addicted to each other. A secret addiction. His wife knew nothing. My family knew I had a boyfriend, but they didn't know he was married. Or a cop. And though Keawe had told one of his friends by now and I had already told Dina and she told Ed, no one else in the department knew about our affair, as far as we knew.

The more intense our relationship became, the more I worked. I didn't want to go home alone and think about him being with his wife. I knew I was in a doomed relationship, but I couldn't make myself end it. On the one hand, I was furious at myself. I was a cop, and here I was at the mercy of a man. Yet all I wanted to do was be with Keawe. He was becoming as important as my work. Maybe more important.

In early May, ten months after my affair with Keawe had begun, I missed a period. We had been careful—I thought we had, anyway—

so I didn't think anything of it at first. I figured it was stress. Working too much, working too hard.

I forgot about it, actually, but a couple of weeks later, I was driving home from work and suddenly felt nauseous.

I pulled over and put my head on the steering wheel until the feeling passed. Lifting my head, I slammed my palm on the wheel.

"Motherfucker!" I yelled. At myself.

I wanted to stop at the drugstore right away and buy a pregnancy test, but I was still in uniform. I stood out on the island—I couldn't risk anyone talking about "the blond cop who bought a pregnancy test"—so I drove home and changed into running shorts and a T-shirt, gathered my hair in a ponytail and put on a baseball cap, and then went to Long's Drugs in Kihei. Filling up a basket with a bunch of shampoo and other toiletries, I headed toward the counter and threw in a pregnancy test at the last moment. I got back in my car but couldn't wait to get home to take the test. Instead, I stopped at the nearest bar, ordered a Coke, and went into the bathroom. I ripped the packaging open and took the test. Three minutes later, I had my answer.

I called Keawe immediately.

"I have something to tell you," I said. "And I need to tell you in person."

"Alli, I can't," he said. "I'm on Oahu."

"What?"

"Yeah, we're visiting Colleen's brother."

"Why didn't you tell me? You didn't tell me you were going."

"I'm sorry," he said. "I guess I forgot."

I took in a deep breath.

"What is it?" he said. "I don't have a lot of time. Can you just tell me?"

I heard the frustration in his voice. "Can you tell me what it is?"

he asked. "I can't do a ten-three now." *10–3:* Maui cop code for "meeting with the girlfriend."

"I'm pregnant," I said.

"*Hapai?*" he said. "How could it be?"

I thought about that word, *hapai,* Hawaiian for pregnant. It sounded almost like "happy," but there was nothing happy about our situation.

"Are you sure?" Keawe asked.

"I'm sure. I just did a test."

All I wanted him to say was, *It's okay, we'll deal with this. I'll tell Colleen everything and ask her for a divorce.*

But that's not what he said.

He said, "We can't—"

"I know."

Keawe was all about being a father. He was a traditional Hawaiian man and though he would want the baby, he wouldn't risk losing his kids. Colleen would probably divorce him if she found out about us, and I didn't want that to happen to him.

"Hey," he said, more gently. "You know I want to."

I tried to squeeze the tears back into my eyes.

"We will someday," he said. "It will be okay. I promise."

I sat down on the couch then and turned on the TV, really wanting to call my mom. She was a great listener. She would have understood. I always regretted not going to her when I got pregnant in high school. Ten years later, I still hadn't told her about that. I would have talked to her now if I could have avoiding telling her Keawe was married. She knew that I had a boyfriend named Keawe, and she knew about my best friend and beat partner, but she had no idea they were the same person. I used Keawe when I talked about him as my boyfriend and his given name, Charles, when I referred to him as my beat partner.

I couldn't tell my mom I was seeing a married man. How could I? Another woman had ruined her marriage, and I didn't want her to know that I was doing that to someone else.

It's not that I even wanted a baby. I was still so young, still in the early days of making a career for myself. It wasn't the right time for me either. But I was furious at myself. All the emotions I had buried for years came out. This was a repeat of high school. How could I be an adult, a cop, and still find myself pregnant and alone?

I had sworn I would never get into this situation again and yet here I was, once more terrified by what I was facing. I wasn't a teenager, I was twenty-six years old. And this was *Keawe's* baby. Keawe's and mine. In my heart I did not want to end the pregnancy, but we had no choice.

I endured horrible morning sickness for three weeks until I could schedule the abortion. In high school, Josh had come to the abortion clinic with me, but Keawe couldn't even do that. Someone would have seen us together, and our affair would have become public.

For a second, I thought about asking Dina to come with me. Since she was in a similar situation with Mankell, she would have understood. But I didn't trust her to keep her mouth shut.

In the end I had my friend Slim drive me. He didn't come in with me, but he dropped me off and picked me up when I was done. He had no idea Keawe and I were having an affair. I told him it was some guy I met in a bar.

In the clinic, when the abortion technician asked me if I wanted to see the ultrasound, I said okay. Big mistake: I turned out to be carrying twins, and she had to ask me if I wanted to terminate both babies or only one.

Both.

Dear God. Both.

I went back to my apartment after the abortion, wanting to die. They had given me minimal sedation, and I was in real physical pain. Far worse than that was my emotional pain. I was furious at myself, furious at Keawe, disappointed with my life. It's almost impossible to describe how much I loathed everything about myself at that moment. Especially the part of me that shut people out to the point that I found myself totally alone when I most needed support. I felt I was having some sort of moral breakdown or betraying my personal code.

I took some painkillers to alleviate the cramping and lay on the couch to watch TV. I was bleeding a lot and could barely stagger to the bathroom when I had to go.

I didn't answer any of Keawe's calls, but I listened to the messages he left. When he showed up that night, I didn't get up to answer the door. He had his own key. I turned my face to the back of the couch when I heard it in the lock.

"How are you feeling, babe?" he asked. When I gave no response, he sat next to me and rubbed my back. I started to shake him off, but the sad truth is, he was the only person who knew what I had just gone through. My only possible ally, though a completely flawed one in so many ways. I needed whatever love and comfort I could drum up. I couldn't risk being angry at him. That would leave me with no one, no one at all.

"I thought you might be hungry," Keawe said. "I stopped at L&L's and got some loco moco."

I didn't answer, and he just sat there. "I feel really terrible," he said. "Do you want me to stay with you?"

Yes, I wanted to say, but of course my answer had to be no. He couldn't stay. I wonder now if I had asked more of him, what would have happened. I wanted to ask more; wanted to say, *Yes, stay with me. Let your wife find out and just deal with it.* But I had learned at an early age not to ask very much of men. I had learned that from my father. Keawe would be sweet to me that night, but then it would be back to business as usual.

The people at the clinic had told me to rest for a couple of days, but I went back to work early the next morning. The painkillers masked my physical discomfort, but I had all these feelings that I didn't want to feel, and there was nothing to mask them.

For once, being a workaholic didn't help. I began to work so much that they wouldn't let me work anymore. If you work six days in a row they insist you take a seventh day off. I got around that rule for a couple of weeks, until my sergeant figured out what was going on and made me take a day off. That day at home was torture to me. I had stripped my life down to the bare essentials of police work and an affair with a married man, and in their absence, I didn't know what to do with myself.

I sank lower.

The next day I felt so depressed I could barely get out of bed. For the first time in my police career, I didn't want to go to work.

But I had to. To cope, I filled a thermos with orange juice and vodka and took it with me to the station. I wasn't even a big drinker. I have no idea where I got that idea, but as soon as I sat down at my desk, I knew I was in real trouble. I went into the bathroom and emptied the thermos into the toilet, then stayed in the stall, crying quietly.

I was screaming for help. That desperate action woke me up, but only temporarily.

For a couple of days after that, I bounced back, but then very suddenly Keawe's shifts and mine changed. We no longer had parallel shifts—now he was working nights while I stayed on the day shift. If I wanted to see him, it would have to be at night, when I was supposed to be asleep.

Night shifts were always slow. He didn't have much to do—usually patrol nights on Maui, you had a couple of hours where it's pretty mellow. Keawe always had rookies working for him, and rookies are really proactive. They would either take Keawe's cases or he would go to his case for twenty minutes and come back to the substation and see me. We were usually together three or four hours in a night.

My new schedule worked like this: I would work in Lahaina from 6 a.m. to 6 p.m., complete two or three hours of paperwork, and go home. After about two hours of sleep, I would get up at midnight and go see Keawe in Kahului. It was an insane schedule, and if my mother had been there, or anyone in my family, they would have told me so. But I was still young and stupid enough to think I was strong enough to do anything.

I was running myself into the ground, running from my feelings. On some level, I knew that Keawe was using me, and I loathed myself for staying with him. But I needed him in the unhealthiest of ways.

I have spent no small amount of time thinking about how everything could have turned out differently if I had sought help at this time. The department had a psychiatrist, but there are old-school stereotypes about talking to a shrink. The fear is they're going to pull you off the job, and nobody wants that. I saw it happen with one of my friends, Manu. He had gotten into a shooting in Kahalui while he was on the job and ended up killing his neighbor. Afterward, he suffered from severe PTSD and they pulled him off the road for a year. It was like a punishment; he was embarrassed by it.

It was an unspoken rule in most departments that you don't just go and talk about your problems. Instead, you fix them by going out drinking with your buddies. I was drowning in my depression, exhausted from lack of sleep, but I didn't ask for help. I had spent my whole life keeping my own secrets, believing that if I didn't tell anyone my story, it couldn't possibly be happening to me.

I also thought a lot about killing myself. Almost daily I imagined how I would do it, mostly quick and easy, with my firearm.

But then another solution presented itself. A couple of weeks after the abortion, I was working with Bergen, one of my beat partners in Lahaina. Everybody knew I was the narcotics girl—that was my niche, that was my thing—and Bergen had a case where a mom in Lahaina had found a packet of ice in her son's room. She didn't want to prosecute, and we couldn't make her, but she wanted to turn the ice over to the cops. Bergen was a great guy but a bit lazy. He couldn't be bothered with it, so he came back to the station and threw me the packet of ice, saying, "You can make this case if you want." He assumed I would file a report because I always did, but this time I didn't.

I put that packet of ice in my pocket and carried it around with me all week. I was never one of those cops who thought they were above the law, but I did recognize the power I had. No one searched a cop. No one questioned a cop. Except for our random drug tests, we were immune. I could carry a packet of ice around with me and no one would ever know.

I decided to risk even more.

I waited until my day off, Saturday.

With all the blinds in my apartment closed, I closed my bedroom door and decided I would try the smallest little line. Just to see how it felt.

I didn't even know how to do it. I knew everything about narcotics except how to actually use. I laid out a small amount, about half the length of a paper clip and very skinny. You're supposed to smoke ice, but I bent over and snorted it.

"Damn!" I yelled. The ice burned my nostrils, and my eyes began to water. I could feel the crystals go up my nose and what felt like into my brain. It felt like the insides of my nostrils were getting ripped out. I grabbed my nose instinctively, as if to stop the drug from entering my brain.

What had I done? I was terrified. So much for my badass behavior. I started to laugh.

But then the pain subsided and the *feeling*, the feeling of meth, the best feeling in the world, began to set in. I could taste the meth running down the back of my throat, a taste similar to that of metal. Bitter, strong, almost sour, but not quite. My jaw muscles clenched. My eyes were still watering, and I felt each tear run down my cheek, but the tears had changed. The release of the water from my eyes was the best sensation of crying I had ever felt.

A wave of enlightenment came over me, a feeling that all was right with the world. A caffeine rush without the jitters; drunkenness without losing control; your first love without the heartbreak. Suddenly I could feel the hairs growing on top of my head. I didn't have five senses, I had thirty! My thoughts began racing:

What do I want to do first? work? clean? go running? wash my car? go to the beach?!!!! there are so many possibilities!!!!! I can bake something for Keawe, do laundry? no, no, no, I can do anything I want to do, I have three days off, I can take an extra shift at work, no I can't go to work high, should I go shopping no don't leave the apartment, this is incredible, I should call my mom, my sister, Mimi, I should call Keawe,

Dina, Slim, no don't do that!!! clean, that is what I want to do!!!!!!!!
I want to clean and organize my entire apartment, yeah, yeah, that is
what I want to do!!!!!

The pain in my nose was gone, replaced by a grandiosity. I was a
much better version of myself. This was going to be great.

8

Keawe came over that night. I greeted him at the door and gave him a deep, lingering kiss. I hadn't given him a kiss like that in weeks. Lately, he had been letting himself in to find me lying on the couch, silent and depressed.

"Wow," he said. "You're feeling better."

"Better than 'better,'" I said. "I feel amazing." I couldn't even remember how bad I had felt just a day before. It was as if the abortion, my anger, my feelings of confusion about Keawe—all of it was suddenly gone. And what replaced it was euphoria.

"I'm relieved," Keawe said. "I've been worried about you."

"I'm good," I said. He had shown up with some take-out chicken katsu from L&L's that he was going to cajole me into eating, but after I had finished cleaning my apartment I had made him his favorite corn chowder and *pani popo*, a Hawaiian coconut bread that he loved. Ignoring all the food, I led him straight into my bedroom, where we had sex for the first time since the abortion.

Ice sex is great sex. You're aroused times eight hundred, and if you feel that great, a lot of it transfers to your partner. Keawe had no idea what he was in for.

"Jesus, Alli," he said afterward. "That was worth the wait."

We ate after that—or he did, anyway. I had no appetite, and I didn't touch the food on my plate. But it gave me pleasure like I had never experienced before to watch Keawe eat with relish the food I had cooked for him.

He didn't want to leave (why would he, after that?), but he was expected at home. Usually when Keawe left I started to feel despair creep over me, resentment and insecurity displacing my happiness, but not this time. Now, I put on some Bob Marley and continued to clean my apartment.

"There's no such thing as problems," I said aloud.

My apartment was immaculate already, but now that I was high I could see how wrong things were, how they must be reorganized. I cleaned my already clean apartment for almost three days. I rarely answered my phone because I didn't have time, I *had* to clean. I cleaned the grout in white tiles individually with a toothbrush and bleach. I steam-cleaned my carpet. I washed *all* of my clothing. Color-coordinated my closets. Alphabetized my spices. Alphabetized everything! Painted my front door.

Also, I didn't eat for three days. Starvation felt good.

When Monday morning came, I hadn't slept a minute, but I wasn't even tired. I went to work.

Work was fantastic that day. I had a couple of traffic stops and then a domestic abuse case, which was unusual for the daytime. But the guy was all coked up and had this idea that he was going to use his girlfriend's head as a crowbar.

Later, I had a meeting with a CI about a buy we were trying to put together. The guy's name was Oscar. He was a punk, a little junkie I had traffic-stopped while on patrol in Wailuku, but he was leading me toward something bigger, I felt. I had been trying to introduce him to Bryant, in vice, who could get at the big dealer more quickly, but most CIs got jittery when I brought someone new to meet them. Oscar trusted me, but that was it. He did not want to meet Bryant. He knew that when he did a buy, it might send up a red flag with the dealer, because if the dealer got popped two weeks down the road, he would remember the one guy they sold to who seemed a little nervous. He was probably going to think Oscar was a CI, and then he would be in big trouble. I spent a lot of time that afternoon coaching Oscar though his next buy, and when we were finished, he was ready to do it.

I was everywhere in Lahaina that day, responding to every call, getting there first. My sergeant actually commented, "You clone yourself over the weekend, Moore?"

I passed the L&L between calls and saw a bunch of cops in there, eating for free, pursued by all the badge-bunny waitresses. I felt nothing but contempt for them. Some of them didn't even bother to put their duty belts on until the call came in. I was working doubly hard and loving it.

After my shift, I followed up on paperwork until nine, catching up on what felt like weeks of work. Then, instead of going home to sleep for a couple of hours like I usually did, I went straight to the substation to hang out with Keawe. We joked and laughed and ate chicken katsu. Everything was absolutely perfect.

I had told myself when I did that line that I would only try it once. I would never do it again. But when I started to come down, I couldn't face being plunged into the icy cold water of my real life. I couldn't bear to have those feelings return. I did another line, bigger than the first. It made me feel calm, confident, excited about my future. Meth was the answer to all my problems.

Along with the euphoria, at that time I was still able to see ahead, to when I would not allow myself to do it again. The faces of meth burned my brain. My thoughts turned to all the meth-related cases at work, my plans for my future, the worries of a random drug test, the shame, the knowledge of having worked with addicts and seeing their behavior. But these logical thoughts were overcome by the effects of the narcotic. No clear-headed thought stood a chance against that one little line.

The face of meth wouldn't happen to me. I was smarter, better, stronger than everyone else. I was invincible.

I bought a pipe and started to smoke the dope, like you're supposed to. I told myself, okay, I'm only going to do this packet, this one packet of ice, and then I'm done.

My time with Keawe was now just how I wanted it to be. We had great sex, some laughs, good hang-out time. Then I would go back to work, where I was supercop. I didn't have to think about the abortion. Or his wife. Or my loneliness. Or anything at all.

That bag of dope lasted me three months. When it was gone, I lay on the floor and cried. I didn't know what to do without it. Ice was the only thing worth living for—I had felt that from the second it entered my body. I needed it to survive the world. Regardless of the fact that it had begun to kill me, ice was now my savior.

9

Now I was an addict, and like any addict I had to figure out a way to get more.

If I had stopped to think about it at the time—if I had stopped to think about *anything*—I probably would have seen that I had always been an addict. Throughout my life, my addiction had never been a substance. I'm addicted to *more*. More work, more control, more exercise, more sex. I'm one of those people who has a bottomless bottom. Whatever it is, bring it on. I will go until I die.

Becoming a cop wasn't a wise decision for me. Addiction is so prevalent among cops because we're trained to suppress whatever anger or emotion we have and stay calm. Where do those emotions go? They go into beating your wife, or they go into exercise, or they go into steroids, or workaholism or alcohol or drugs. Since I had entered recruit school exactly three years earlier, I had put everything into work.

Now it was the drug.

There was no way for me to get ice on Maui. Too many of the dealers knew me; I would be busted instantly. If I wanted to pick up, I would have to go to another island.

I was familiar with Honolulu because I had done some training there in my rookie days. I knew where to find the prostitutes and crackheads, and they would lead me to dope.

That Friday night, I took the 10:50 p.m. flight to Honolulu, rented a car, and drove to Hotel Street, where the prostitutes work. Most of the Chinatown prostitutes are beautiful, but I spotted one who looked like she really needed some work. I drove up next to her and opened my window.

"Hey," I called. "Want to get in?"

She turned toward me. Thin as a rail with skin as wrinkled and leathery as a Florida grandmother's, she was probably thirty-five but looked past fifty. A crackerjack, easy to spot.

She didn't hesitate before getting into my car. As soon as she was sitting in the passenger seat, she said, "What you got in mind?"

She didn't look at me while she spoke. She had a huge bag with her, almost like a homeless person's bag.

"Looking for ice," I said.

She nodded. "What you gonna pay?"

"You use?"

She nodded. "Rock."

"Fine." We agreed that she would buy ice for me if I would buy her some crack. I gave her a hundred bucks and dropped her off near a gated doorway on River Street.

"I'll leave my bag," she said, "so you know I'm coming back." A cop car was parked directly in front of me. They were all over Hotel Street and Chinatown, but they're mostly there to keep the peace and collect "taxes," not to arrest anybody. I sat listening to Tool on my iPod while she went inside.

She came out a few minutes later with my ice, and we drove to another location to get her crack. After that, I drove her back to Hotel Street.

"Can I look for you again?" I asked her.

"Almost always here," she said. "If you don't see me, ask for Angel. Everybody knows Angel."

After dropping Angel off, I drove to Waikiki Beach and parked at the Honolulu Zoo. No one was around, and I walked across the street to Queen's Beach, sat on my jacket in the sand, and smoked ice. I smoked all night until it was time to drive to the airport.

I caught the 5:50 a.m. flight back to Maui and was back home by 8 a.m. No one in Maui even knew I was gone.

When I walked into work Monday morning, I saw Dina and another female officer, Erin, talking quietly. They stopped when I came up to them and turned bright, fake smiles on me. I could tell they had been talking about me. My meth paranoia was already kicking in, and I was sure they had somehow figured out what I had just done. Still, I tried to make light of the situation.

"You talking stink about me?" I asked them.

"Choke." Erin laughed. The Hawaiian expression for *a lot*. All three of us were *haoles*, but we had embraced the Hawaiian language. Erin's eyes darted around the station. "Let's go outside for a sec."

We stepped out into the bright Maui sunshine. This is it, I thought. They were about to tell me that they knew about my using. I quickly formulated my strategy. I would tell them that yes, I was using, that I had tried ice once to get closer to one of my dealers and hadn't been able to stop. I would plead with them to keep it a secret. I didn't know much about Erin, but I knew Dina wouldn't judge me. She was my friend. She knew what went with the territory.

"We're worried about you," Dina began.

Her words brought me a little relief. I couldn't stop on my own, that much was clear, but they would help me. I could wipe the drug out of my life, like it had never existed.

"We've noticed you're getting really thin," Erin was saying.

I knew I was losing weight, but this was the first time anyone had mentioned it. You don't eat when you're using meth, and even if you do eat, your metabolism is running so fast you can't keep weight on. I had even had to buy new uniform pants.

Dina said, "You told us you were anorexic when you were a teenager. We're worried you might be going down that road again."

I searched their faces, trying to figure out if they were really trying to get at something else. They looked sincere. And concerned.

"I know I'm getting thin," I said. "I've just been so stressed. With work and everything."

"You're a ripper," Erin said, "and everybody knows it, but there's limits, girl."

"You have to start taking better care of yourself," Dina said.

"I know," I said. I was touched by how caring they were. How they really wanted to help me. MPD takes care of its own. For maybe ten seconds, I considered telling them the truth—one of many times I thought about coming clean to somebody. But of course I didn't.

"Come out with us after work tonight," Erin said. "Have a burger and a milkshake."

"We'll fatten you up," Dina said.

"Sure!" I said, enthusiastically. "I'd love to come. Thanks, guys." That was my usual tactic—agreeing to attend a social event and then not showing up. Or dropping by for a few minutes at most—just long enough for people to know I had been there.

True to form, after work I texted Dina that I would try to stop by, but instead I worked late at the station and then went home for a couple of hours. I needed to fit in a hit before meeting Keawe.

After Erin's and Dina's comments, I tried to gain some weight by eating as much as I could and drinking a lot of protein shakes, but Keawe mentioned my weight loss too, a week or two later.

"Have you been talking to Erin and Dina?" I asked him.

"Nah, but you're losing your curves, babe. Your *okole* is getting bony," he said, slapping my ass. I was surprised that he would notice. Generally, he liked me thin. His wife was thin, and it made me happy to be thinner than she was.

I started making the trip to Honolulu with some regularity. I carried the ice in my jeans pocket when I was flying back and forth, oblivious to what would happen if it was discovered. I didn't worry about getting searched by security. I had my badge, but also, when you're using you feel like you're untouchable anyway. I never got caught. Once I left my ice packet in the rental car and when I went back for it, two guys were already cleaning the car.

"I think I forgot something in my car," I said.

"No," one of them said, and snickered. "We didn't find anything." Both of them started laughing, and I knew they would be smoking my ice as soon as they got off work. *Assholes.*

Every time I flew to Honolulu, it was the last time. Every time I got a packet of ice, I told myself it was the last packet. In reality, I was using more and more. At first I'd go to see Angel once a month, and then it became every three weeks. Seven months into using, I was making the trip every two weeks.

My drug use was progressing, but my work was progressing also. Because I wasn't sleeping, I was working all the time. I dug deep into the narcotics network; people began to trust me and I was building up a CI base.

I was getting lots of praise at work, and letters of commendation from the chief about my cases. I needed three years on patrol before they could promote me, and I had only six more months to go. With all my narcotics work, I was a shoo-in for vice.

10

My birthday fell on a Saturday that March. I knew Keawe had the day off so I scheduled a day off for myself too. As the week went on, I kept waiting for him to say something about it. He knew the date, and though we hadn't done much for my birthday the previous year, this year I was fixated on it. Keawe and I had been together for eighteen months now, and I expected more from him.

My friends at work bought me a little cake on Friday and sang to me. I told everybody I had plans for Saturday and sat home alone, waiting for Keawe to call. My mom called. My sister called. My aunt and Mimi and a couple of my cousins called, and I told all of them that I was celebrating later with a bunch of friends. A lie: I had no friends, except my fellow cops. What girl in her twenties doesn't have friends? All I had was work. And meth. And work. And more meth.

And, I thought, Keawe.

By evening, when I still hadn't heard from him, I knew I wouldn't. My meth paranoia had started to kick in, and I decided that he was punishing me, that he had found out about my ice use and wanted to make me pay for it. I had been smoking meth all day and now smoked even more. I paced around my apartment, wanting to throw things, wanting to jump off the lanai. I couldn't stop thinking about Keawe, and about another man who wouldn't be calling on my birthday. My father, Ian.

I was twenty-seven years old and hadn't seen him in almost eight years.

After my father moved out of our house when I was in high school, he hid from our family, keeping his new address and phone number a secret from us. He didn't want my mom knowing where he lived; he wanted to keep as much distance between them as possible. All I had was his work number, which his secretary answered, so in order to see my father I had to make an appointment with the woman he left my mother for.

It was horrible. I was a teenage girl who wanted her father to love her, and he had no time for me. I refused to have that kind of relationship, so when I was nineteen, on Father's Day, I found out where he and his secretary/girlfriend, Claire, were living and I showed up at the house. It was a beautiful walled home in the Albuquerque country club area. I was furious to see him living there while my mom was struggling to pay the mortgage each month.

The house had a little stream running through the front yard. A fucking *stream*. To reach the front door, I had to go through a gate and walk over the bridge that crossed the stream.

I was all dressed up in nice suit pants and a black sweater. I rang the doorbell and of course *she* answered.

"Oh, hello," she said.

"I want to talk to my father," I said. I held a Father's Day card for him in my left hand.

He came down and we all stood awkwardly in the foyer.

"Happy Father's Day, Dad," I said, and handed him the card.

"Thank you," he said.

"I need to talk to you." I glanced at the secretary. "Can we talk alone?"

"I have no secrets from Claire," he said.

"Please," I said. "It's really important."

"Alli," he said. "What is it? I don't have a lot of time."

But we were so close! I wanted to shout at him. *I was a daddy's girl!*

"Let's go sit down in the library," Claire said.

We walked down the hall and through a kitchen that seemed to be made all of copper—copper sink, copper island, copper pots hanging down from a rack on the ceiling. In the library, there were hundreds of books on the built-in shelves, but they didn't look like books anyone would read. They almost looked color-coordinated, chosen for their covers and not what was inside.

"Sit down," Claire said. She and my father sat side by side on a plush loveseat and I sat across from them on an uncomfortable upright chair. A ridiculous-looking cat jumped on Claire's lap and she sat there petting it while they both stared at me.

"Well," I said nervously. "It's just about our, our relationship. I need it to be different."

My father didn't say anything. I glanced over his shoulder and saw a picture of me on the mantel. *You fake fuck*, I thought. *How dare you have a picture of me in your house when you wouldn't even tell me where you live?*

"I miss you, Dad. I want to see you more. I want to be able to call you directly instead of making an appointment," I said. "I want you to call me and ask me out to lunch." I poured my heart out to him in a way that I hadn't done before. I had always kept my thoughts to myself. All the while Claire glared at me, and my father sat there like he was obligated to do so.

Glancing around the room, I saw pieces of furniture that had been in my grandfather's house. My grandfather—my father's father—had been a wonderful man, and I had loved him, but as he got older, my father had frozen him out of the family business. When he became unable to take care of himself, my father left him in a caretaker's house across town. He died alone, and my mother, sister, and I hadn't been welcome at his funeral.

What right do you have to his furniture, you fuck?

My father stared at me, giving no reaction. When I finished talking, he said, "It sounds like I can't give you the kind of relationship you want."

"What, Dad? Why?" Tears welled up in my eyes.

"I just can't give that to you. There's no room for that in my life."

"There's no room for *me* in your life?"

"I guess that's all I have to say," my father said.

"I better go." I got up and walked to the door, fighting tears.

As I left, my father tried to hug me. When I was little, he had been very affectionate with my sister and me. He had given great hugs. But now, I thought, *Hug me? After you told me you didn't want me?*

I crossed over the stream and back to my car.

Sobbing, I drove back to my mom's house. I cried and cried in her arms all night and never talked about it again. My mom would ask me about it now and then and I would completely close down. I detached from that day, from *him*, but I always felt so hurt by what he had said to me.

After that day, my father and I never spoke. The odd birthday card came, usually signed by *her*, and for my twentieth birthday he had sent me a Swarovski crystal bear—Swarovski was a passion of Claire's, so I knew she picked it out, not him. Every year, I held out hope that he would call on my birthday. My mom sent him emails updating him on my whereabouts, my activities, but he never replied. He and Claire moved to Florida, but we only found that out much later. He hadn't called when I graduated from the academy. He hadn't called at all.

I hadn't seen or spoken to him since that Father's Day almost eight years ago.

"Asshole," I yelled, not sure if I was addressing Keawe or my father.

To calm myself down I started speedballing—taking Oxycontin and mixing it with meth. I had seized the oxy on a traffic stop, and I took it to try to mellow me out, but it just made me crazier. I'm not an opiate person. Uppers are my thing. I thought I was going to die a couple of times during that weekend because my heart was beating so fast. Finally I got smart and stopped the Oxycontin, but my withdrawals were insane. I stayed home from work on Monday and was really sick. So sick I couldn't even smoke meth for a few days. But in the end I thought, *If I can get off the Oxycontin, I can quit meth any time I want.*

Keawe called me on Monday. "Hey," he said. "I didn't hear from you all weekend. Whatcha been doing?"

"It was my birthday," I said.

"Oh shit, I forgot!" he said, and I could tell by the spontaneous way he spoke that he was telling the truth. "You must be so pissed at me, Alli. Geez, I'm sorry."

"It's okay," I said.

"I'll make it up to you," he said. "I'll get you a present. We'll celebrate."

"Great," I said. *Right*, I thought.

Shortly after my birthday, I made a trip home to New Mexico to see my granddad, my mother's father. He was terminally ill with lung cancer. He had been diagnosed in the late fall and had been given a choice: no chemo and he would be dead within three weeks, or chemo and the possibility of six months. We were all happy that he had chosen chemo. We were in month five now, and with no one really able to predict how long he was going to live, I knew I needed to spend some time with him in Albuquerque.

It was the first real break I had taken from work since I started at MPD.

I was high the entire time.

"I need more time, Alli," Granddad told me as we sat in the courtyard of his house, soaking up some early April sun. He glanced across the courtyard at his studio and nodded sadly. Granddad had been a professor of architecture, but later in his life he had become a painter of some renown.

"I still have ideas for paintings I want to do. There's just not enough time."

I didn't know what to say to that.

"Do you like your work?" he asked me.

"Yes," I answered. "I love my work."

"That's good. Me, I wasted too many years. In my heart I was really a painter. It's important to find out what you are in your heart."

"I guess I'm a cop in my heart," I said.

He nodded wisely. "I guess my granddaughter is smarter than

I am," he teased. "Me, I wasted too much time filling my life with things I didn't want to do."

It was painful later to think I was high during that time. I knew that this would be the last time I saw him, and I felt such shame as he told me how proud he was of me. *No*, I wanted to say. *I'm not smarter than you, Granddad. I'm a drug addict.*

My shame catapulted me into extreme using. I had figured one packet of ice would last me through my whole trip to Albuquerque, but it didn't. After a few days I had to go out looking for dope.

I took my granddad's nice Subaru and drove down East Central, heading into the projects, where I clearly didn't belong. The War Zone, we called it. I found a prostitute who introduced me to a pimp who said he could get me some dope for two hundred dollars. I gave him the two hundred and he gave me a plastic baggie, but when I opened up the plastic bag, I saw that all it contained was the powder residue from crack pipes.

I was so desperate, I snorted the residue. My nose burned so badly I thought I would have to go to the ER. My right eye felt like it was going to pop out of my head.

I drove around a little bit longer, until I saw a woman smoking crack. When I asked her where she got her dope, she introduced me to her pimp, who found me some ice. It wasn't as good as the ice in Hawaii, but it got me through.

Another prostitute introduced me to a guy who gave me dope but also took me to the casino. I wasn't willing to prostitute myself for the drug—I still had money—so I just obliged him by going to the casino with him all night. In the morning I got home just before everyone was getting up. I took advantage of my mom's alcoholism. She would pass out at seven, my grandparents would go to bed at nine, and I would be out and back home in the morning before they got up.

I lost that time with Granddad. I know he would be proud that I'm sober now, but I wish I had been then. Or I could have used that time to talk to him about my addiction. He knew all about addiction.

Granddad had been sober for more than twenty years at this point, but Mimi offered him a martini one night. "I'm sure it's okay," she said. "It can't matter now."

"No," he said. "I don't want to miss a single minute."

When I left, I gave him the tweed newsboy cap I had been wearing all week. He had admired it. "I don't need it," I told him. "You have it." I was pleased that I could give him something, even if it was such a silly thing. He was wearing tracksuits at that time, and the last I saw him, he was wearing a purple velour tracksuit with that tweed cap, sitting at the kitchen table with a blanket on his lap.

I went home to Maui and swore off dope, vowing that Granddad would live and I would get sober. I actually stopped using briefly and started to gain some weight.

Two weeks later, I got the call that Granddad had died. I turned around and headed back to Albuquerque. The department was very understanding. I had already taken time off to visit him, and they were happy to allow me another week to go back to his funeral.

I had some sober time at the funeral. My cousin Ken was high on heroin at the funeral, but not me. I barely fit into my clothes because I was gaining so much weight.

I thought I had beat it. I was hell-bent on living in the right. I was done. I was never going to pick up again.

And I was going to stop my affair with a married man. When I went back to Maui, I planned to break it off with Keawe. I had been so upset that Keawe couldn't come to the funeral and thought, *That's it. He's not here when I need him. Ever. It's over.*

But without meth I felt exhausted, tired, emotional. I felt I couldn't handle the situation with Keawe without it. In classic addict behavior, I used Granddad's funeral as an excuse to pick up.

I relapsed pretty hard while I was in Albuquerque that second time. I could only take two hundred out of the ATM every day, so I stole a thousand dollars from my mom and went and gambled. I lost it all and then the next night I stole another grand and won it all back. I spent eight hundred one night on crack and meth with a crackhead and made up some story about how the car got towed and I had to get it out of the yard and pay all these fees.

I came back to Maui after the funeral and really wasn't able to put together much clean time. Maybe a week here or there when I thought there would be a drug test. Or a couple of days. Instead of stopping using, I began to speedball and mix dope.

Things were spiraling down with Keawe, too. My behavior was more erratic. I wasn't generally a yeller, but I started having fights with him, yelling on the phone and calling him names, which is never right to do with someone you love. I made it really difficult for him, and he didn't understand what I was doing.

And then one Monday morning, I walked into a drug test. By this time, I had mapped out the pattern of the department's supposedly random testing—usually every third month, toward the end of the month. Rarely on Mondays. Around then, I would cut back on my using and drink as much water as I could, trying to flush the drug out of my system. Meth withdrawals made me extremely tired, so I would ramp up for them by taking massive quantities of every kind of legal upper. Caffeine pills, NoDoz. So far I had passed all the tests. I started to get nervous. I had been lucky and knew it was only a matter of time before my luck would run out.

This test had come sooner than I expected.

A few hours after the test, I started to hear rumors in the department that someone had tested positive. I knew it had to be me. I figured the best thing to do was to own up, so I headed down the hall to talk to the chief. My meth paranoia convinced me that this unexpected test was orchestrated all because of me. They knew—everybody knew—and all they needed was proof.

Walking down the hallway, about to be caught, I was in some ways relieved. I would be done. No more lying, no more hiding.

"Hey, Alli."

I turned to see Slim motioning me over to his desk.

"Did you hear?" he whispered. "Klemm tested dirty."

"Klemm?" I asked.

Slim smirked. He had never liked Klemm. Across the room I could see the chief at Klemm's desk, motioning him to stand up. Slim and I watched the two of them walk down the hallway past us and into the chief's office. The door closed behind them and we all knew what that meant.

Klemm was one of the Wailuku patrol guys. He was into narcotics work too, and had wanted to get into vice, but he tested positive for ice that day and was forced to resign.

The same drug test that he failed, I passed. Klemm got fired, and within the month, I was promoted to vice.

11

One Friday morning, I got called out of patrol to meet with Assistant Chief Patrick. Patrick was an asshole by all accounts, but he ran the vice division of the department so I had worked hard to stay on his good side.

He was smiling when I entered his office.

"Alli, come in, come in," he said, sounding strangely jolly. "I gotta tell you, Alli, you didn't give the best panel interview—"

"I know, sir. They nailed me with some very difficult questions." The panel had asked me the HRS number for a Schedule II drug, and I had gotten it wrong. I had walked out of the interview positive that I'd blown it.

"So your interview wasn't so hot," Patrick said, "but you are the most qualified officer for the position. Your record speaks for itself. I wanted to meet with you personally to make sure that you accept this position."

"Position?" I said, confused.

"Vice," he said. "We want you. You want us?"

"Yes. Yes, sir!" It started to sink in: I was being promoted to vice.

"But I need to ask you this. How do you feel about being the only female in the division, Alli?" he asked.

It pissed me off that everyone in the department called me by my first name. They would never do that to a guy.

I tried to answer Patrick's question. "It comes with the territory," I said. "I was the only female on Lanai. The only female in Lahaina."

"Lahaina has Peters on patrol."

"She's been on injury leave since I've been there," I said.

"Right, plus she's a *tita*," he said, using the Hawaiian term for dyke. I had met Peters once or twice; she was fairly big and masculine-looking, but I hated the label.

Patrick suddenly became very stern. "I expect a lot out of you, Alli. We've never had a girl in vice before, and you'll need to prove yourself."

"I will," I said. I started to launch into a long speech about how this was my dream, how I would do my department proud, how I would—but he cut me off.

"You've got two weeks left in patrol before you're assigned to me," he said. "The staff doesn't know yet, so you'll have to keep quiet."

"I got it, sir."

I walked around with that secret for two weeks. Kid stuff compared to the bigger things I was concealing from my friends and colleagues. It was hardest not to tell Keawe. He had been against my applying for vice right from the start. Vice comes with a bit of prestige and a bigger paycheck, and that wasn't what he wanted for me while he was still a patrolman.

He was the first person I told when Patrick gave me clearance. As I suspected, he wasn't pleased.

"I don't think you can handle it, babe," he said. "Patrol is one thing, but vice—those are real guys' guys. They're not gonna let you into their club so easy."

"I'll have to make them," I said aggressively. His negativity pissed me off. "I'll show them I can be one of the boys."

To join vice was to move up in the department—literally. The vice office was on the second floor, above patrol, and patrolmen would rarely get to go up there. I was issued a bunch of cool vice equipment, all brand-new, and a Glock .27, smaller and more compact than patrol's Glock .22. All the vice officers and detectives used a .27, and the patrolmen were jealous. Most cops have nicknames for their weapons, and I called my new Glock Gunther.

Vice was such a creative division. You could work as hard or as little as you wanted in vice, but everyone who got promoted to the division was a workaholic like me anyway. I had to show up at the office at eight thirty to appease the brass, but after that my day was mine to plan. Total freedom. Nobody was checking up on me, so I could make my own cases.

And find places to smoke dope with greater ease.

Keawe was right—it was hard being a female coming into the division. Vice guys were beer-drinking, adrenaline-fueled, women-loving men. They accepted me to a certain degree, but at the same time I was always an outsider.

Early on in vice, I was assigned to work surveillance with one of my partners, Maliko, assisting the FBI in an important case. I was a little nervous about working with him. He was an okay cop, but he was one of Keawe's best friends, and one of the few people who knew about our affair.

On our first night doing surveillance together, he brought his PlayStation Portable with him.

"Anything special you want to watch, Alli?" he asked me.

"No, but is now the time to be watching movies?"

"Now is definitely the time. We can't do anything yet anyway."

We were waiting for a call from command post to tell us where they wanted us staged, but sometimes unexpected things happen during surveillance—a third party shows up, for example, or there are lookouts. You really have to be on point.

"But—" I started to say.

"Trust me on this, Officer Moore. I've been around awhile."

I was pissed when Maliko started staring at his PSP. I felt we needed to be on our A game when working with the feds. I later found out all the other vice guys had PSPs.

"I can put something else on if you tell me what you want to watch."

"I don't care what you watch," I said.

"You're a cool chick," he said.

A minute or two later, bored, I looked over to see what he was watching.

Porn.

Jesus.

My mind started racing, and I didn't know what I was going to do. Instead of kicking his ass or telling him what a fucker he was being, I just laughed and said, "You're a riot, Maliko."

I felt so uncomfortable. He didn't make a move on me or anything, but he continued watching for about an hour until we got the call from the feds.

Later that week, Maliko told me jokingly, "I think I'm addicted to porn."

I should have said, *You think? Get some help, you fucker.* But I wanted to be cool, so I said, "There's nothing wrong with watching two people make love, but you should probably talk to your wife about what's going on with you."

"Are you kidding?" he said. "I could never talk to her about this. She's a conservative type. Not like you, Moore. I can talk to you about anything. That must be why Keawe likes you so much."

I was concerned that Maliko was hitting on me, but at the same time I took pride in the fact that I was *one of the boys*. In that situation, I thought agreeing with Maliko, making him feel comfortable with a somewhat serious problem at the cost of my feelings and morals, was what made me fit in.

I made men feel that they could be themselves around me, that I would be cool with it. I did the same thing with Keawe. He told me that at home he was stifled, but that he loved being around me because I was accepting of everything he did. I made the mistake of thinking I was showing him true love. In reality, I was confusing being a yes-man with unconditional love.

Now that I was in vice, I was finally doing what I had always wanted to do: focusing on narcotics, getting them out of the community. My career had become less about the law and more about community, and I remembered what had drawn me to MPD in the first place—my love for the island and its friendly, welcoming atmosphere. Vice only made me more of an advocate for the community I loved. I still believed that narcotics were the root of so much crime in Hawaii—property crime, domestic violence, theft—and

I still wanted to eradicate drugs from the islands. I just wanted enough left for me.

I understood what a hypocrite I was being, but I didn't care.

In one of my first assignments for vice, I got to be part of the marijuana eradication team (ERAD). Off Piilani Highway there was a military airfield hidden in the cane fields. Everyone knew about it, but it was rarely used except by MPD. We had to coordinate with the DEA and helicopter pilots from Maui and Oahu to send out helicopters over Maui, Molokai, and Lanai.

First up was being fitted for my flight suit. That was one of the best days ever, all *Top Gun* with MPD vice patches and flight patches all over the suit. Because they had never had a female vice officer before, they had to scramble to find a suit small enough to fit me. I felt like such a badass.

We worked out of three helicopters—two large military DEA helicopters and one smaller model that ran interference for us, checking for any dangers on the ground or in the air. Armed men, for example, or telephone wires.

We flew all over the three islands to harvest marijuana from the cane fields and lava fields below. It was gorgeous. The islands looked so lush and green, the ocean lively and blue. I almost forgot we were on a mission. I got caught up in the view until one of my partners yelled, "I've got something!"

We rappelled from the helicopter down a thick yellow cord into the marijuana fields. With machetes, we cut away the marijuana plants. It was hard work, really hot, and we got covered with marijuana tar. Once we'd harvested the field, we wrapped the plants in ropes and hoisted them up to the helicopters, stuffing them inside the cab so we could fly back to the military airport to burn them.

I was the last one left on the ground, and just when I was expecting to be pulled back into the helicopter, they let me hang there in my harness, dragging me lightly over the tops of the trees.

"Welcome to vice, Officer Moore!" the guys yelled down at me, laughing. It was my initiation onto the team.

"Woohoo!" I yelled, waving one arm at them while holding on for dear life with my other.

Marijuana eradication team was an amazing experience for an adrenaline junkie like me. It should have been the time of my life, but all I kept thinking was, *How can I fit in a hit while I'm up here?*

12

By this point, all my money was going to ice. All of it. The flight to Oahu was $200, renting a car was another $100, and I would pay Angel $200 for my dope and $60 to $100 for hers. I didn't have $600 to spend every two weeks, and my bills were falling behind. I was broke. I pawned a video camera I had and would have pawned other things but I didn't have much to begin with. I was always working and wasn't a very materialistic person. Before I knew it I was calling my mom to help me pay the rent.

Finally, I was left with only one choice: I was going to have to stop paying for my dope.

Being in vice made that easy.

I turned to my CIs. After they made a buy with a drug dealer, they'd bring me back the dope. Before sending it to the evidence locker, I would skim a bit off the top, then weigh and submit what was left. No one was any the wiser.

Skimming off the top of my CIs' buys was a new low for me. By using, I was breaking the law every day, but in my mind I was maintaining some degree of morality until I started tampering with department evidence.

My using was getting heavy. If I got up at midnight, I would do a hit, go see Keawe, then do a hit in my car before work. After work I would do another hit so I could drive home without falling asleep at the wheel. I also kept ice in my pocket to smoke in the bathroom of the station. I had carefully undone the stitching of my tennis shoes, and that was where I kept my pipe.

As my using progressed, so did my efforts to hide it. I had an ice bump on my thumb from holding down my lighter to light a pipe. I wore a Band-Aid over the bump and told everyone I had a hangnail. I wore colored contacts to conceal the size of my pupils, which got so wide my eyes looked black. I chewed gum all the time—even though ice has no smell, I was paranoid that Keawe would somehow taste it when he kissed me or get some sort of residual high.

There wasn't a lot of room for Keawe in my life at this point. He came third after the drug and the job, and though he didn't know about the drug, he was pissed when I ignored him. He wanted me available whenever he was and called me way too often. I would set my phone to vibrate, and often the phone would ring off the desk when I didn't answer it after his many calls.

I was terribly, terribly thin, but I wasn't getting the face-of-meth look like you saw on the posters hanging on bus stops all over Maui. I wasn't a picker, I didn't have sores, my teeth weren't falling out. I was lucky. Lucky, or unlucky? Maybe if I had showed some of those outward signs earlier, someone would have figured out what was going on with me. I could have gotten some help.

Later, I found it hard to believe that no one suspected I was using. My family was so far away, but how could Keawe not know?

Or Dina? Or Erin? They saw me every day. All my MPD colleagues were trained to recognize drug use—why didn't they recognize it in me? Looking back on this time later, I sometimes found myself angry at them for not seeing what I was taking such great pains to conceal.

Why didn't one of my goddamned drug tests come back positive? How was I able to pass every single one?

A couple of months into vice, there was rumor of another drug test coming and I tried to flush the dope out of my system. Withdrawals took me down hard and fast this time. I was supposed to meet Keawe at work at midnight, as usual. He called all night, but I didn't hear the phone. I slept for twenty-four hours straight, and when I woke up I discovered that I was two hours late for my shift. I had never missed work before, and I was scared.

I called Wilkes immediately.

"Moore!" he said. "Where the hell are you? We've been calling and calling."

"You were?" I asked. "I didn't hear."

"Hell, yes. I was about to send a patrolman out."

"I'm so sorry, sir," I said. "I overslept. I can't believe it. I was just so tired, I've been working so hard—"

"We all know that," he said. "Jesus. The hours you keep, I'm amazed this is your first no-call/no-show."

"I understand there will be disciplinary action," I said. "But I'm on my way right now, and I'll finish out my shift."

"Of course. Listen, I'll go easy on you since this is your first time." He was teasing me, I could hear it in his voice. He wasn't going to do anything. "Just don't let it happen again," he said, sounding like some teenager's dad.

"Got it, sir."

I scrambled to get ready, knowing I wasn't in real trouble—yet.

Everybody knew how hard I worked, how strong my arrest record was. They weren't about to come down on me for something like this. I knew cops who routinely had to be called in after late nights and parties, but I did not have that reputation. I would be fine.

When I hung up the phone, I realized I was trembling. I reached for my ice pipe. I couldn't function without the stuff. Damn any drug tests—there was no way I could justify stopping.

Meanwhile, I had a new CI, a huge Samoan dealer named Kal who I'd gotten through working with Oscar. I'd carried Oscar into vice with me as an informant, and we had been working our way up the drug tree together for a while until we got to Kal. I executed a search warrant on Kal's house and car and found about an eight ball of cocaine. An eight ball isn't very much, but it turns out that Kal was a big-time player and also involved in the organized crime on Maui. I managed to flip him, and he was about to introduce us to a big dealer in Kihei who was moving pounds, but for now he was still doing buys for us.

One buy that Kal did brought in a huge packet of ice. When I took it from him he shook his head sadly and said, "I'm sorry to see this go. This is the best, purest shit you'll ever get."

I couldn't wait to smoke it.

I didn't want to bother fitting work around my dope schedule, so I made up the lie that my mother had died and I had to go back to Albuquerque to her funeral. MPD had been so nice when my granddad died that I knew they would give me the time off.

I called my sergeant to tell him. "Jesus, Alli, that's horrible. Take all the time you need."

"I'm sorry," Keawe said when I called him. "You must be feeling terrible. Can you come see me before you leave?"

"No, I have to leave right away," I said. "This afternoon. I'll call you when I get back."

Erin was off that day and came over as soon as she heard the news. With a cake. A *cake*.

"I'm so sorry," she said, hugging me. "Do you want me to come with you? I've got some time off coming. You shouldn't make a trip like this on your own. Jesus! Your *mother*."

"No," I said. "I mean, thanks, but I'll be okay. My family is really supportive."

"Take care of yourself, okay? You look awful. Which is under-standable."

There was no reason for anyone at MPD to disbelieve me. No one knew a thing about my family—that's how isolated and secre-tive my life had been. It was an easy, easy lie.

I took five days' bereavement leave. Everyone thought I was in New Mexico, but I never left my apartment. For five days, I didn't drive my car or open the blinds or leave to buy food. I ate Erin's cake and some Ritz crackers and yogurt and whatever else I had in my cabinets, which wasn't much.

I did nothing but sit there and smoke meth for the entire five days.

Best five days of my life.

13

My ability to lie is a skill I wish upon no one. I am a chameleon in the worst way: I can slither and adapt to suit the needs of anyone I want something from. This is what made me a good cop. I was able to appeal to anyone I came in contact with—my superiors, my CIs, my worst criminal offenders—and build a rapport with them almost immediately. Everything about me is inviting, trustworthy. I appear innocent.

I placed a lot of faith in lies. They could save me, sustain me, keep me shielded from anything that threatened me.

Even myself. Especially myself.

And they came to me as easy as breathing.

When I was fifteen and came to in the helicopter after driving myself off the cliff in Tijeras Canyon, the first thing anyone asked me was whether I had tried to kill myself. My lie, automatic, was: *It was an accident, I was driving too fast.*

Instead of dealing with the feelings that had led me to that cliff, I lied away their very existence. I detached completely from my suicide attempt, telling no one about it. Ever. My lying turned the suicide attempt into an accident, even in my own mind.

In movies and books, certain characters always attempt to draw others out of their isolation, trying to get them to open up, to share the truth. Real life doesn't work like that, at least not in my experience. Most people are happy not to deal with someone else's shit. *Keeping it locked up inside, that's your strategy? Works for me.* So when people ask how I kept that secret for all those years, I tell them it wasn't hard at all. I'm a good liar, and nobody really minded.

And now, when I was a newly minted vice cop and a dedicated meth addict, my lies began taking on a breathtaking life of their own. They shot out every which way, joining together to create the rickety scaffolding that was supposed to be my life.

My mother died. I need to go to Albuquerque.

Easy as breathing.

By necessity, my lie about my mother dying spawned another lie. In early December, my mom called and said, "Alli, we want you to come home for Christmas. It's been too long! We really miss you."

"I can't, Mom," I said. "I just can't. I'm working on this huge case." That wasn't a lie—Kal and I were closing in on a big dealer in what was the biggest case of my career, and one of the biggest cases Maui vice had ever handled.

"Come on, Alli," said my mom, who always had a dramatic sense of occasion. "It's Christmas!"

"I don't have a choice. I need to be here. Now that I'm in vice, things are different. And AC Patrick is kind of an a-hole about stuff like that."

"I get that," my mom said. "But everyone needs family time at Christmas. Can't you get away for just a few days? I can't stand thinking of you being all by yourself during the holidays."

"I'll be fine," I said. "I'll probably be working the whole time."

"I'm not happy about this," my mom said.

"I'm sorry," I said. "I just can't leave."

I should have chosen my words more carefully because my mom called three days later with another plan.

"Guess what?" she said, sounding happier than she had in a long time.

"What?" I said.

"Mimi and I are coming to spend Christmas with you!"

"You are?" I asked uncertainly.

"Yes! Since it's the first Christmas since Granddad's death, everybody thinks it would be good to give her a change. Get her away from home. Too many painful reminders here."

"Do you really think that's a good idea?" I asked cautiously. I was starting to panic. "Does Mimi even want to come?"

"It was her suggestion," my mom said happily. "And a brilliant one. I don't know why we didn't think of it sooner."

"So when are you coming?" I asked.

"A week before Christmas. And leaving New Year's Day. I've got lots of time off coming to me. It's not a problem."

Two weeks! My heart sank. How in the world would I keep my using from them for two solid weeks?

In the past, I had loved when my family came to visit. I had begged them to. This time, I did everything I could to discourage them.

"Do you really think Mimi's up to the trip?" I asked my mom.

"She needs it," my mom said. "This will be the hardest Christmas of her life."

"I know, but she's so . . . frail."

"She's stronger than you think," my mom said. "It'll do her good."

I tried another tack. "I just don't know how much time I'll have to spend with you," I said. "I'll be working all the time."

"Do you *not* want us to come, Alli?" my mom asked sharply.

I had to lie to avoid hurting her feelings.

"Of course I want you guys to come," I said. "I mean, gosh, I'm so excited."

Inwardly, I thought, *Oh shit*.

Everyone thought my mother was dead. How would I keep her presence a secret from Keawe? He had a key to my apartment and would show up whenever he wanted.

I would have to fabricate a very special lie for Keawe.

"I need my key back temporarily," I told him the next night when I went to see him at work. He was working on his own, as he was most nights. He sent his rookies out a lot and was very choosy about his cases. He had a reputation as a complainer in the department, but he always got what he wanted.

"Your key?" he asked. "You breaking up with me?" He smiled, joking.

"I'm going to be away over Christmas, and I told my landlady that nobody would be using the apartment."

"Sure," he said, removing my key from his key ring and handing it to me. "But where are you going?" As far as he knew, I had nowhere to go. My parents were dead (I had told everyone long ago that my father was dead), and I never took vacations.

"Well, I wasn't going to tell you this," I said. "It's kind of embarrassing. It's just that, my family—my sister and my aunt and my grandma—they think I've been working way too hard. They're worried about me."

"Everyone knows you work way too hard. My little ripper."

"Yeah, well, they think I need help. Mental help."

"That's extreme."

"I guess so. But they know me pretty well, so . . . Anyway they're sending me to a mental facility for two weeks."

"Jesus," Keawe said. I wanted him to rush in with concern, to say *I had no idea things were that bad; what can I do; I'm here for you, babe.* Instead he said, "Well, if you think it will help."

That was it? No outpouring of support? No requests for my family's contact information? Not even any commonsense questions, like, *Where is this "facility"?*

"Yeah," I said. "Whatever."

Just then a call came in. "I gotta go," he said. "You'll call me when you can, right?"

"Right," I answered, the bile rising in my throat as I watched him walk away. We were in the station so of course he couldn't kiss me or show any sign of affection. Even so, his indifference chilled me.

I had sent out a desperate cry for help to Keawe. A cry that he didn't answer.

On a day before my mom and Mimi arrived, Erin came over with an armful of Christmas gifts. I didn't tell her the mental institution story, but she knew I wasn't going to be around for Christmas.

She handed me six or seven nicely wrapped packages that she couldn't wait for me to open.

I hadn't gotten her a thing. I looked around my apartment, as if a tree and presents would miraculously appear out of nowhere. I had done nothing to prepare for the holiday.

"I'm sorry," I said. "I didn't—I haven't had a chance to get to the store—"

She brushed me away. "I know you're really busy with work," she said. "I didn't expect anything. I just saw a couple of things that made me think of you."

Erin was such a generous person, a straight shooter with a Boston accent and a heart of gold. She'd been trying for a while to make our friendship more than it was, and I had resisted. For one thing, she drank too much, and I had no interest in hanging out in bars. But more than that, she was just one of the many people who passed through my life without my really seeing them, knowing them, because I was so focused on using and work.

I was happy to see my mom and Mimi when I picked them up at the airport that Christmas, but within a day I just wished they would leave. They wanted to go out for dinner all the time, visit tourist spots, sit and talk for hours on end. They insisted on buying a tree and decorating my apartment for Christmas. They wanted to take me Christmas shopping every day.

All of this interfered with my using. And it got old very quickly, listening to them tell me how I was too thin, how I worked too hard, how I was young and needed to get out and have more *fun*.

After three days I couldn't stand it. I told them I needed to travel for work, and of course they believed me. They had an enormous respect for law enforcement and didn't really understand the particularities of what I did. They would have believed anything I told them.

I flew to Oahu and checked into the Queen Kapiolani Hotel, where I could smoke meth without having to hide it from anybody. I called Keawe every day or so, pretending to be in a mental health ward.

"Be sure to listen to the doctors," he told me. "Don't be combative. Just try to relax and you'll get better in a few days."

To make my situation seem realistic, while I was on the phone with Keawe, I would pretend the orderlies were asking me questions and then pretend to answer them. Sometimes I would scream at these fake orderlies. "I'm getting off the fucking phone!" I would yell. "Just leave me alone!"

It was insane.

Keawe didn't have much to say about my situation. It seemed he didn't know what to say, and looking back, I still don't know what he was thinking. Most likely, he thought I was crazy, but if so, why did he keep calling me, talking to me? Why didn't he break things off? It didn't make any sense.

Every time I got off the phone with him I felt this hole in the center of my chest. His lack of reaction devastated me, but what did I expect him to do, really? Rescue me from my fake institution?

After more than two years with Keawe, I felt like I was starving for love. He had made all these broken promises to me. Sometimes when I think about him now, I wonder if all my lies, even the worst of them, were just desperate attempts to get him to be with me. It's like those mothers who try to make their children sick just to get attention for themselves.

It's terrifying to think that I would do that, that lying would come so easy to me.

I've carried this character defect of lying throughout my life. At times I have justified it because of my job—the need to be versatile, to make friends with everyone from police sergeant to junkie—but it's something I've been struggling with in all areas of my life.

I know exactly where my lying comes from.

My father.

I share a lot of his traits—the lying, the manipulation, the detachment. It makes me ill. All I ever wanted was to be nothing like my father, and now I had become the spitting image of him.

My mom liked to say that that my father learned to "approximate" normalcy. He was an exceptional imitator, a shape-shifter who could take on the appearance of any group as needed. Just like I did.

My mom blamed his detachment on the polio he had had as a child. He was a victim of the last viral wave to strike the United States in 1948. He spent from age two to age five in Texas hospitals, much of that time in isolation wards. It had a disastrous effect on him, we found out, and eventually all those around him. He didn't experience the human bonding and socializing that we all need. Polio left him with a weakened leg, but his biggest loss was that human spark that ignites connections from one to another. Throughout his life, he cut people off—first his closest friend, and then his father, and then later his family.

It had been eight years since I'd seen him.

In a way, when I told people that my father was dead, I was telling the truth.

As I sat in that hotel by myself in the days leading up to Christmas, juggling my lies to Keawe with my lies to my family and to the department, I tried not to think about my mom and Mimi back in Maui, driving around the island like tourists without me—to Haleakala, up to a luau in Lahaina, out on the Hana highway. But I did think about them. And I also thought about my granddad, and how I had spent my last time with him high.

No quantity of meth could make these feelings go away. I just wanted to die.

Actually, I had two moods at that time: high and suicidal. On one particular day, the suicidal took over and I tried to figure out how to kill myself. Unfortunately I didn't have my firearm with me, and the Queen Kapiolani didn't have a lanai to jump off, so I had to find another way.

I broke a glass from the bathroom and used the jagged edge to cut my arm open. Sitting on the tiled floor of the hotel bathroom, I watched my arm bleed for a while. The cut was deep, but not deep enough to kill me very efficiently. The pain didn't bother me, but the boredom did. It was tedious waiting to die, and I still had some meth left to smoke. I made a tourniquet from the hotel towels and smoked meth until the bleeding stopped.

Later, I put a bandage on the wound, and when I got back to Maui, my mom asked immediately, "What happened to you?"

"Oh, this," I said, waving my arm as if such things happened to me all the time. "I was on a case. This dealer tried to run, and I had to climb over a chain link fence to chase him. I snagged my arm."

"Oh my gosh," my mom said. "Let me see."

"It's nothing," I said, though it actually was pretty substantial. I should have gotten stitches—it ended up giving me a permanent scar.

"Have you had a tetanus shot?" Mimi asked. "You don't want to get an infection."

"The hospital took care of that," I said, though of course no one but me had looked at it.

My first night back in Maui, I crashed, and for the rest of the holidays, all I did was sleep. We made it through Christmas, but then my mom got annoyed with my endless sleeping and she and my grandma ended up leaving early. I felt terrible about that—my poor little eighty-year-old grieving grandma—but also I felt relieved because I needed to get back to smoking meth.

As soon as they left, I called Keawe and told him I was back. He came to my apartment that night and the first thing he said was, "What happened to your arm?"

Weirdly, I told him the truth. I looked him in the eye and said, "I tried to kill myself."

He was visibly shocked but didn't seem to know what to say.

"How?" he asked.

How? Not why?

"At the institution, I broke a glass and cut my arm."

"They let you have glass in those places?" he asked. "You'd think it would be too dangerous."

"I guess," I said.

"But you're better now, right?" he asked, and what could I do but nod my head.

I was sick and I was looking for him to rescue me: *Leave your wife for me, I'm so miserable, I'm so ill.*

But he wasn't going to rescue me. When Keawe left that night, I had the small realization that he wasn't going to save me. Nobody was going to save me. I would have to save myself.

I swore to myself that I would quit. I would stop disappointing my family and become the me they used to know. I was done with ice. No more.

I put together two sober days before I was back to smoking ice. I couldn't survive without it.

Keawe was working on New Year's Eve, and the night before he asked me, "So what you doing for New Year's?"

I didn't want him to think that I would be home by myself doing nothing. I needed him to think that I had all sorts of friends and a social life.

"I've got a party to go to," I said.

"Nice. Think of me stuck here working."

"Too bad for you."

"Come see me before you go," he said, and smiled. "Please."

And so I got dressed up for New Year's. I bought a new dress, put on lots of makeup, straightened my hair.

"Wow," he said when I walked into the substation that night. "I'd like to be going to *that* party."

"You wish," said Maliko, who happened to be in the station.

I spent about a half hour talking to Keawe and then went back to my apartment. I had nowhere to go, absolutely nothing to do. I might have called my family to wish them a happy New Year, but it was too late in Albuquerque now. Still, I justified it to myself: *If Keawe believes I have a social life, it's enough for me.*

Waiting for midnight, I sat around in my tiny black strapless dress, smoking meth, completely alone.

My addiction was taking me down hard and fast. I had become skilled at hiding it, but it got to the point when nothing would work. I looked sick. The ice was eating me from the inside out, and sooner or later everyone was going to find out.

It was going to take a big lie to buy me a little more time.

One morning Sergeant Wilkes called me into his office and said, "Moore, you look so thin, you look like you're dying. Do you have cancer?"

That was just his way of joking, but a new lie had presented itself, a ready-made lie invented by someone else.

"Yes," I said. "I do have cancer. That's why I'm so thin."

"How long have you known?"

"Since November."

Wilkes nodded thoughtfully. "And when were you going to tell us?" he asked.

"I honestly didn't think you needed to know," I said. "I know I can beat this thing. I don't want everybody feeling sorry for me."

"You know there's not a man in this department who wouldn't be there for you if you needed us," he said.

"I know that, and I'll ask for help if I need it, but for now I'm okay. I just don't want anybody to know. Please don't tell anybody."

"You don't have to do this on your own," he said. "We're your brothers in blue."

"I know."

"What kind of cancer is it? What's the"—he searched for the word—"prognosis?"

"Ovarian," I said. "The prognosis isn't great long-term, but I'm doing fine now."

Where did I get this stuff? Things I had read, I guess, or heard on TV. I sounded utterly convincing.

Understand that at this point, I would have done anything to keep my addiction alive. Anything. Wilkes just happened to be there, and the comment that slipped out of his mouth became my new best lie. If it hadn't been Wilkes, it would have been another colleague, another lie.

Although I pleaded with him not to tell anyone, I knew he eventually would, and before the news started to spread like wildfire I would have to tell Keawe.

I told him the cancer wasn't serious, that I would be okay.

"You don't look like you're getting any better," he said.

"I am," I said. "The treatments are working and it won't be long."

As usual, Keawe didn't have much to say, but he held me close and told me he loved me. I would have to settle for that.

Yes, I have cancer.

When I started to face these people, to look them in the eye and tell them I had cancer, as I started to do that January, this was the moment my lies became deceit and my deceit became premeditated actions that I knew, *knew* would cause pain. Never mind all the horror that happened later, lying to the people who loved me held more pain than anything that would ever happen to me physically.

You look terrible, Alli. Do you have cancer?

Yes, I have cancer.

That was beginning of the lie that would take me down, that would destroy the trust of a whole community on the island.

14

At first, the cancer lie was great. I now had permission to look as sick as I actually was, and if I didn't want to make it into work, I could take a sick day.

We were conducting a couple of really big investigations at the time, and one of them went federal. The FBI needed my report, but I just couldn't get it done. I was in the bathroom smoking every thirty minutes. Even though a hit of meth lasts fifteen hours, I still wanted more. I would get higher and higher and higher at work, thinking that if I could just take one more hit I could sit down and do this report. I couldn't. I kept telling everyone my cancer wasn't serious, but I was clearly falling apart, so Wilkes suggested I take some time off.

"Don't you have some family to go visit?" he asked me. "I know your parents are gone, but isn't there a sister in Oregon?"

"Washington," I corrected him.

"Why don't you go spend a couple of weeks with her?"

"I'm working on this no-dope warrant with a CI," I said. "I need to be here to—"

"No, you don't," he said. "Bryant can fill in for you."

I opened my mouth to protest further, but then I started to think about it. My big case was pretty involved and included all nine vice officers. My CI Kal and I were narrowing in on the Kihei dealer. There was no undercover work—it was all done via surveillance and CI buys. A no-dope warrant. Kal had made three small buys for us from this dealer. I had done two of them, and now Bryant was ready to do the last one because I wasn't capable. I just couldn't concentrate, couldn't get any work done, and we were close to having the warrant ready to be executed.

"There is this great oncologist in Seattle that my sister has been telling me about," I told Wilkes.

"Sounds good," Wilkes said. "Visit your sister. Rest. See this cancer doctor. Get well."

Biggest case of my career, and I listened to Wilkes and left for Washington to visit my sister. Can you effing believe it?

Now the entire Maui Police Department thought I was on the mainland, getting treatment for my made-up ovarian cancer. Instead, I was at my sister's house in Seattle, trying to buy dope online.

I still had a little money but was about to run out of ice, so I got on Craigslist and used the key words for finding the dope I wanted. Cocaine users say, "Does anybody want to go skiing?" All I had to ask was, "Has anyone seen my friend Tina?"

First I looked for gay guys. Much safer—they wouldn't want sex from me. In the drug world, a girl's money is no good. You can try to pay for it, but you're not going to get very far. You might be able to pay half. The other half you've got to earn.

I was lucky. I found a gay man named Evan who didn't have any money but was willing to introduce me to his dealer if I would share with him.

That night at eleven o'clock, after my sister, brother-in-law, and two little nieces had gone to sleep, I sneaked out of the house. Just like high school. Evan had told me to meet him in a warehouse parking lot, but when I pulled up in my sister's Subaru there were no other cars there. I took a hit of ice and waited.

Out of nowhere this guy knocked on the window.

"Shit," I said, thinking it was a cop.

"Hey, Alli. I'm Evan."

"Where did you come from?" I asked. "Where's your car?"

"I kind of walked," he said. "My parents usually don't let me take the car."

"How old are you?" I asked, opening the door and letting him in.

"Twenty-five."

I had a quick look at him before the door slammed shut and the car went dark again. He was dressed in a blue shirt and khakis. His brown hair was nicely cut. All-American Seattle boy. Handsome. Twenty-five, but he looked sixteen.

"You live with your parents?"

"Yeah," he said. "They put me in rehab like a million times and it never worked. Now they won't give me any money. They think that's going to keep me from using."

We drove about fifteen minutes to a small brick house in a quiet neighborhood. Evan had me park a few houses away.

"This your dealer?" I asked him.

"Sure, he's a dealer."

I was a little confused because online he made it sound like he had his own dealer, tried and tested. I gave him a hundred bucks, and he disappeared inside the house.

After about ten minutes he came running out.

"Drive," he said. "Just drive."

"Don't do that," I said as we tore down the street. "Don't steal from a dealer. You'll get known."

"I saved you some money," he said. "Now we've got enough for tomorrow night, too."

"Jesus," I said. At work I had seen more than once what dealers did to buyers who tried to rip them off.

"It's okay," he said. "God, you drive fast. Let's go to my house."

He directed me to an upper-class neighborhood near my sister's house in Snohomish. A really beautiful house. His parents' house.

And inside—his parents. June and Ward Cleaver. His mother in a dress. They were smiling, smiling. They seemed like they wanted to chat, but all we cared about was getting high. Evan said, "This is Alli," and hurried me upstairs.

"Will they kick me out?" I asked.

"They never come up here," he said. "This is my part of the house. They're down there having orgasms over you. They're pretending you're my pretty blond girlfriend."

"They don't know you're gay?"

"Oh they know, but they don't accept it. They're super fundamentalist Christians and they think I'm going to hell." He smiled a sad sort of smile. "I probably am. Going to hell."

"So where's the dope?"

He pulled a baggie out of his pocket. "How do you use?" he asked me.

"I have a pipe."

"Ever slam?"

I shook my head no.

"I slam. Want to try?"

"No thanks."

We sat on his bedroom floor and I watched him shoot up while I smoked. Once we were high, he put on Sarah McLachlan.

The whole second story of the house was his. His room was total ADD—some books were neatly shelved while others were open on the floor; a big mound of clothes sat in a corner but inside his open closet, pants and shirts and sweaters were grouped by color. There were no sheets on his mattress. It seemed that in typical tweaker fashion, he started a lot of projects but couldn't concentrate enough to finish them.

After Sarah McLachlan, he put on Fiona Apple. Then he took me across the hall to the computer room with a giant LCD monitor, Internet, and television.

"This is where I really live," he said, pointing to the computer.

We played video games together and he started talking to me about women's stockings.

Turns out he was a cross-dresser. He had some women's clothes in his closet but nothing really beautiful. He really, really loved pantyhose.

"They must feel wonderful on your legs," he said. "So soft and silky."

"I hardly ever wear them," I said.

"Do you have some? Could you bring some to me?"

"I guess," I said. "Sure."

"Do you think they'll fit me, even though I'm a guy?"

"Why not?"

"What size do you think I'd wear?"

"I don't know, maybe medium tall?"

"But not queen-size, right? I mean, I'm thin."

I nodded. He was desperately thin. As thin as I was.

He wanted to talk about stockings all night. I could see it made him feel good, and I didn't mind.

"It's not like I want to be a woman," he said. "I just want to dress like one. I just want men to think I'm beautiful. You think that's weird, don't you?"

"No," I said. "You should do whatever makes you feel good."

"Nothing really makes me feel good. Except this." He nodded his head toward the bag of meth.

We talked all night, this tweaker Chatty Cathy stuff, and at dawn I drove back to my sister's house, where everyone was still asleep. They never even knew I was gone.

I had enough meth with me now to smoke all day while Carol and Tim were at work and Ella and Maya were at day care, but I knew I'd run out in a day or so. I looked around my sister's house for things I could sell. Her golf clubs. Some of Tim's tools. Things they might not miss, at least for a while. I put them on Craigslist to see if I would get any takers. I had a really expensive vice camera with me that had "County of Maui" engraved on it. A thousand-dollar camera, and I went out that afternoon and pawned it for a hundred.

While I was driving back from the pawnshop, Keawe called.

"Hey," he said. "Whatcha doing?"

"Nothing," I said. "Doing some shopping for my sister."

"Are you up to that?" he asked. "What does the doctor say?"

"There's this terrific oncologist here," I said. "She's suggesting some new treatments. Really, I'm getting better."

"Babe, I hope so because I want you back now. I miss you so much."

I continued to throw all sorts of little lies at Keawe, but my heart always lifted when I spoke to him. For a while our relationship had been perfect for me because I could be a workaholic and not have to handle someone who wanted to take me away from work. I had been blindsided by the loneliness and guilt and disappointment that came from being in love with a married man. But even now, though I couldn't speak to him without lying, my love for him was true.

Carol came home from work with Maya and Ella and bags and bags of groceries. I helped her empty the bags onto the kitchen table. Boxes of organic granola and containers of yogurt, bags of fresh fruit.

"You're looking pretty thin, Alli," Carol said. I froze, a loaf of brown bread in each hand. If she had noticed how thin I was, she had to suspect I was using. The cancer lie was for the department alone—for my family there would have to be another one.

"Your pants are practically falling off you," she continued. "Let's go shopping tonight. Let's get you some new jeans."

This was my big sister—take-charge, generous, always looking after me. "You know," I said, "I would love to, but I'm watching my expenses now so I don't want to buy anything new."

Carol waved her hand in my face. "My treat," she said. "Let's pick out something for your birthday."

My birthday was more than a month away.

"Oh thanks, but really, I don't need anything. I just didn't pack the right clothes for this trip. I don't know what I was thinking."

"One pair of jeans?" she said. "Please? Otherwise I don't know what I'll get you."

I could imagine what shopping with my sister would be like. My sister coming into the dressing room and seeing how thin I really was.

"That sounds great," I finally said. "But can we do it tomorrow? I've got a really bad stomachache. I think I'm going to lie down."

Carol was used to my stomachaches, my headaches. My sickliness. It had been there all my life, some ailment or another, more since my father had left. Carol was the strong one, the manager, the organizer, sometimes too much the taskmaster. Even losing her leg in the accident hadn't changed her basic approach to life.

I went into my room and took a hit, felt better. I kept the door closed, kept myself really high. I could hear my nieces running around laughing, shrieking, playing. I paced for hours while the household went through the motions of dinner, bath, bedtime. After a while I turned off the light so Carol wouldn't knock on the door, and as soon as I knew everyone was asleep, I took off for Evan's.

Same thing, different dealer. I told him, "You give the guy the money this time or I'm not sharing with you." My addict's logic—I could steal from my sister, but I wasn't going to rip off some drug dealer.

I had brought Evan some stockings and a cute little outfit—a low-cut, ruffly purple top, a tight black miniskirt, something really provocative—and he loved it. I dressed him up like a girl and put some blush and eyeliner on him.

"Look at us," he said. "We're like the homecoming queens." I caught sight of us in the huge mirror he had over his dresser. He was right. I was way too thin and frail, but for better or for worse, I didn't look like the meth addicts you see on posters all over Hawaii. My skin was okay. I'd avoided those horrible staph infections. I hadn't become a picker. My teeth weren't rotting. I was twenty-seven years old, but I still had the look of a teenager. And Evan, he was skinny too, but dressed up he didn't look like the horrible addict he was. For tonight he was the gorgeous girl he wanted to be.

After we got high, we walked around a deserted park near his house. It was two, three in the morning. For him, this was the ultimate. In our crazy drug relationship he felt he could be himself

around me. He told me he didn't fit in anywhere. His parents refused to accept him, and his whole life was lived online, talking to
other gay men. I was the first person who had told him it was okay
to be a cross-dresser.

My third night with Evan, I let him shoot me up. My first time.
I had never used with anyone before and I had always been too
scared to try it by myself.

"I don't know what I have, Alli," Evan said. "Hep-C, HIV. I have
no idea." I waved his words away with my arm, then held it out for
the needle.

The drug felt strong and pure and scary. I loved it.

I wanted more slamming.

Worried that my sister would wake up one night—maybe Maya
or Ella would have a nightmare and call out for her—I told her I'd
received permission to work with the Everett Police Department on
one of their narc ops. I'd be gone most nights. Of course my sister
believed this. My family seemed to be in awe of my police work.
I could tell them anything. This excuse explained my nighttime
absences and also gave me permission to stay in my room all day,
smoking meth while I pretended to sleep.

For five more nights I went to Evan's to share dope with him.
Every time, his parents smiled. They didn't seem to care that I was
coming over at eleven at night and leaving at five in the morning.
They pretended I was his pretty girlfriend. They knew about the
meth and hated it, but they didn't kick him out. He was their only
child, and they were going to let him stay with them until he killed
himself.

When I was in rehab, people would associate all their good
times, their partying times, with meth. For them, that was the hardest part of being sober—missing the drug life and the crazy drug
friendships. I was such an isolated user that I never had that; this

time with Evan was the closest I ever came. He told me he loved me, and I told him I loved him too. As messed up as it all was, I gave him a forum where he could talk about himself, where he wasn't trapped in an Internet world. For a week we were each other's best friend.

Each morning when I left Evan's, he made me take the dope-filled needles home with me. "I don't want to steal from you," he said, "but if I'm alone with the dope I will. I'll use them if you don't take them."

And so I would take these needles to my sister's house, where my nieces were two and three years old and into everything. I wasn't careful—they easily could have found the needles. One time I washed a pair of jeans that had a packet of dope in the pocket. I didn't care that my sister could have found it or that Ella could have chewed on it. I was just pissed that I might have lost the dope.

Paranoid that Carol would see the needle marks on my arms, I began wearing long-sleeved blouses over long underwear shirts. I wore rubber bands at the wrists of the long underwear so that the shirts would not ride up. Going shopping was now out of the question, so I made sure that my stomachaches persisted. Soon Carol was driving to all the Walgreens and CVSs all over town looking for the right antacids for me. I know she was worried about me, but to this day she swears that drugs did not enter her mind.

All during this time I was leading a double life with my sister and her family—sneaking into my room to smoke meth during my niece's third birthday party, using fifty dollars to buy her a present and then resenting her because I would rather have spent that money on dope.

Not just a double life, but a triple life, on the phone with the department and with Keawe, telling them I was doing better, getting stronger, that the cancer wasn't that bad.

"When are you coming home?" Keawe would ask eagerly.

"Soon," I would say. "Soon."

"Do you want me to come to Washington?" he would ask. "Do you need me there?"

We both knew I couldn't say yes because there was no way he could come. But it made me feel better that he asked.

And with MPD. Bryant called me and told me they had to move on the warrant, and I was so high I didn't care that I wasn't there. I had been convincing Kal via long-distance phone calls to trust Bryant and work with him, and he finally agreed he would.

The warrant resulted in the recovery of a couple of pounds of cocaine from the dealer's house, nothing major. Then, in a twist, Bryant was able flip the dealer, resulting in the seizure of a storage container holding over ten pounds each of cocaine and meth. A huge seizure, and then the DEA took over.

I received all sorts of praise and respect from my guys in vice and became the division's newest hotshot. Too bad I was so strung out I didn't care.

So Keawe and all of Maui thought I was dying of cancer, my sister thought I had stomach problems, and the only person who knew anything resembling the truth was a cross-dressing fundamentalist Christian tweaker I had known all of a week.

I probably would have shot up with Evan until it killed him or me or both of us, but I started running out of money for dope and Evan didn't have any. His parents paid him to volunteer at their church, and that's where he got the little dope money he had. He would also rob people, dealers especially. He prostituted himself out, not really caring whether he got paid or not. He just wanted some man to love him. It's rare that anyone who uses meth, homo- or heterosexual, doesn't turn to prostitution. You reach the point of desperation and you don't feel the emotions that you would usually feel in that situation. If you're doing heroin or cocaine, you're still feeling something. You'll feel fear or shame. Not with meth. Also, meth hits the same part of the brain that gets hit with an orgasm, only times a thousand. You're so sexual. Taking that next step to prostitute yourself really isn't hard and most people in the meth world don't condemn you for it. Everybody does it.

The last night I saw Evan, I stole eighty dollars from my sister's ATM and we went to pick up some new dope. Back at his place, he shot me up. Right away I knew something was wrong. I felt a gurgling in my throat that reminded me of critically injured people I had seen on patrol who would aspirate. Evan's eyes widened in panic. I knew I had overdosed.

"Oh God, Alli, are you all right?" Evan took me in his arms and lay me down on the bed.

I couldn't speak. I couldn't move. Obviously he wasn't going to take me to the ER. Instead, I lay on his bed, terrified that I was about to die. For six hours I tried to stop my heart from exploding. Evan lay with me, stroking my hair and holding me.

"I love you," he said over and over again. "I love you so much, you're going to be all right. I'm going to stay with you. I'm going to take care of you." He stayed with me all night and never used the meth himself. I was sure I was going to die, but by dawn it was over.

Evan took me downstairs and helped me into the car.

"I'm glad you're all right, Alli," he said, hugging me.

Later I thought about his parents, sleeping downstairs while a girl was overdosing on their second floor.

I never saw Evan again after that night. Though I would like to say it was because of what happened, that I was horrified or ashamed or something, it was really because of money. I had run out, and he didn't have any. Now that I couldn't use him for dope, I didn't need him. He called and called my cell phone that day, leaving messages, asking me if I was all right, and I ignored them all. Finally he called my sister's house so I had to talk to him. I essentially broke up with him over the phone and that was the end of our beautiful tweaker bullshit love story.

I'm sure Evan's dead by now. He had already surrendered to the drug.

And I was about to.

All it took was meeting my last dealer.

15

After the overdose, I swore I would never pick up again, but later that night I was back on Craigslist.

I found a guy who would be willing to give me dope if I had sex with him, and I went down to the Seattle airport area to meet him at a seedy hotel. He looked like a normal family man—forties, glasses, thinning hair. He actually looked kind of *tired*—and that comforted me somehow. I also worried that he might be a cop.

We smoked meth together and had sex. It was easy and fast. It didn't make me feel like a prostitute. I didn't cry after. I didn't even think about it. Later, yes, but right then meth was suppressing all my normal human responses. All I cared about was getting dope.

He gave me a very tiny amount so that I would have to meet with him again right away. After that first night, he wouldn't pay for a hotel. He lived an hour south of the airport, and my sister's house was an hour north of the airport, so we would meet in a warehouse parking lot and have sex in his car. I preferred it that way anyway. In vice, we liked to arrange stings or drug buys out in the open, where you could run. Once you were in a residence, there was too much opportunity for trouble.

This man was pretty nice, but he was hard to get ahold of, and he never gave me very much dope.

The next man I met with, same thing: he looked like a normal family man, not a tweaker or a drug addict. He was kind of pudgy, midforties, really nice car. I gave that guy a blowjob and then he gave me a baggie. Meth has all these nicknames. It's called crystal, Tina, glass, or shards, and when I was chatting with him online we were using the code word glass. So afterward, when he gave me this baggie, he said, "Here's your glass," and I saw that it was a bag of actual glass shards.

"Get the hell out of my car, you cunt," he said.

That time I did break down, but I can't tell you if it was because I felt like a real prostitute or because I didn't get the dope.

I met with a couple of other different guys, always in parking lots, did the same thing, and was able to get a tiny bit of dope. I had unprotected sex with these men, every single one of them. I didn't think about AIDS or STDs or Keawe. I had gone from being a cop who wiped down her police belt with sanitizer every night to an ice whore.

Then I began to have trouble finding guys with dope, but I met a guy who was willing to pay me for sex. I met with him in a parking lot and gave him a blowjob. The deal was for sex, $250 for sex, but we stopped after a blowjob. He paid me anyway and after that he called me constantly, wanting to meet again for sex. But I had already gotten my money and was looking for dope, so I never called that guy back or saw him again.

I had been gone from Maui for two weeks when Wilkes called. I had run out of vacation time and was eating into my sick days. He asked me for a doctor's note.

"Sure," I said.

"We should have gotten this from your doctor here, but if you're seeing someone in Seattle now that's good."

"I'll get it right away," I said, "and bring it back with me."

"Can you fax it?" Wilkes asked. "We need it right away. I'm sure it's the last thing you have time for now, but—" He sounded uncomfortable and I let him talk for a bit before I said, "Okay, no problem. I'll fax it to you."

The whole time we were talking I was on the computer looking up random Washington doctors online. When I found an oncologist with a good website, I cut and pasted his logo onto a Microsoft Word document to create the doctor's note. I printed it out and forged the doctor's signature before faxing it to Wilkes.

Money for sex was easy to get, but dope was harder. I was always on the Internet, trawling, hoping to find one steady supplier.

Finally, I found him.

I met him on Craigslist after all the other men.

Earlier that particular night I had gone to meet a different guy, but he didn't have any dope so I was headed back to my sister's house with the money I got for a blowjob. A man called and I agreed to meet him. He said his name was Craig. I had been emailing with so many guys, I had no idea which one he was, what he looked like, if he was a cop, a murderer, anything. And I didn't care. All I wanted was dope, he said he had it, and I knew what I had to do to get it.

We met for the first time in his red truck in a valley near my sister's house. The truck reeked of nicotine but was otherwise clean and well cared for. He looked about the same as the other guys—white, bald, about forty, nondescript. But big. And strong. He wasn't thin and weak like most meth addicts. He told me he worked as a specialist carpenter, and that's how he kept his muscles. At first I thought he might be a cop or a fed, but when he smoked meth with me I knew he was neither.

We had fast sex in his truck. I spent maybe twenty minutes with him.

"I don't have much dope on me," he said, "but if you come back to the house we can fix that."

"Thanks," I said. "I'm good." I knew better than to go to his house.

He had great dope, and back at my sister's house I was craving more of it. I emailed him, setting it up to meet him at his house that night. I knew by his mannerisms, the quality of meth, and how he had it packaged that he was a dealer. And a dealer was what I wanted.

That night, I drove to the address he gave me in Everett. I knew it was stupid going to a dealer's house, but at that point I didn't care. Or mostly didn't care. I cared enough to write his name and address on a small piece of paper and leave it in my sister's house. I guess I thought if something really bad happened, if she didn't hear from me right away, she would search my room and find the address and know where to find me.

Outwardly, the dealer's house was just another suburban split-level. Well kept, with good landscaping, on a quiet cul-de-sac in a nice neighborhood. I surveyed the neighborhood before I went in. It was the perfect location for a drug dealer. Around the back of the house were some woods and a lake as opposed to another house or street—any kind of surveillance would have been very, very difficult for law enforcement. For him, monitoring the street traffic would be easy, and if he ever had to run, he could go on foot through the wooded area behind the house.

I was already sensing that he was highly intelligent for a dealer, especially for one who used meth. Usually dealers don't touch the stuff because it interferes too much with running the business.

He opened the door as I came up the walk.

"Hi, Alli," he said, as if I were an old friend coming for a visit. "You found the house okay?"

"Sure." I nodded. "Good directions."

He led me inside. The place was clean and well decorated and definitely didn't look like any drug house I had ever busted. Little did I know the horror of that house.

In the living room there was a leather couch and two easy chairs. A guy about the dealer's age sat in one of the chairs. On the couch was a girl, maybe a year or two younger than I was.

"Joe and Tiffany," he said. "This is Alli." It sounded like he was introducing me as his girlfriend.

"Hi," I said, starting to sit down in the second easy chair. Everything felt so weird, like a goddamn party.

"Why don't you sit next to Tiffany," the dealer said.

Tiffany moved her feet so that there was room for me.

Okay, I thought, he's a CI and these are cops. But that couldn't be right. We never arranged a sting in someone's house.

Then a pipe was produced, and I started to relax. The dealer let me have one hit, then motioned for me to follow him upstairs.

I counted four bedrooms upstairs, and he led me to his at the end of the hallway. A tabby cat wafted by us. I love animals, but I prefer dogs to cats. Still, I bent to pet the cat.

"What's her name?" I asked, but he didn't answer.

I figured he was either a married man whose family was out

of town or a pretty decent-size dealer. What man needs a four-bedroom home? It definitely didn't seem like a bachelor pad.

I fucked him to get the dope and then we smoked together. He gave me as much as I wanted, which I loved.

Toward dawn, I said, "I've got to get going."

"I don't want you to leave," he said. "Stay here with me."

"I'd like to, but I can't. I have to get back to my sister's before she wakes up."

"Stay."

I shook my head. "I'll come back, though," I promised. "I'll come back tonight."

He gave me enough dope to smoke during the day, and I made it home before anyone was up. My phone rang as soon as I walked into the house.

"Shit," I said, trying to silence it. It was him.

"I miss you," he said. "I want to make sure you're coming back."

"I said I'd be there tonight," I said, annoyed. He was starting to remind me of one of the other guys I had met online. I didn't need somebody who wanted companionship, a girlfriend. I needed dope.

"What time?"

"I don't know. Late. Eleven or twelve."

"Alli?" my sister said, flipping on a light in the dark kitchen where I stood. "Who is that? Why are you on the phone so early?"

"I gotta go," I told the dealer, and then turned to Carol. "It's the Everett PD," I told her. "There's a big vice case they've got going down this week. It's going to be most nights, I'm sorry to say."

"Do you have to?" Carol asked. "We barely get to visit with you."

"It's an awesome opportunity," I said. "The chief has me in line for sergeant, you know. This is exactly the kind of stuff I need to do to show him that I can make it." Carol was looking at me oddly, and for about the thousandth time I thought, *She knows; she's about to tell me she knows.* "Of course if it's inconvenient," I said, "they'd be happy to put me up in a motel."

It worked. She bought it. "No, don't do that," she said. "You know you're always welcome here. I just—miss you, that's all. It's like you're here and you're not here." She moved to hug me, something I tried to avoid. She could *see* how thin I was. I didn't need her to *feel* it too.

I smoked all day at Carol's, and when I got to the dealer's that night, it was wonderful. I liked his dope, and unlike the other guys, he gave me all I wanted.

He seemed to want me to be his girlfriend, so I acted the part. It was easy enough to do, and if it got me more dope, great.

I carried on for four or five nights like this. Sometimes Joe and Tiffany were at his house when I went over, sometimes just Tiffany, sometimes different people. They all seemed to be drug friends, nothing more. Tiffany was about my age but lived with her parents, on probation after failing a drug test. She was always asking me for money.

As the nights went on, I learned a little about his business. He didn't own the house, so nothing of his could be seized if he ever got busted. He was a long-term renter, and he had the owners over now and again to show them the renovations he did. He kept them happy, and they didn't suspect a thing. He never sold from the house, though sometimes he had people over to negotiate. He would leave at odd times to "do a deal." He only had one bank account and kept very little money in it. I didn't know where he kept the cash. I couldn't figure out where he kept all the dope, but he was very careful to never keep more than an ounce in the house. He kept all the paraphernalia separated and in different areas of the house where it would blend in. He stored the dollar baggies in the shop where he had little parts and screws that the baggies could be used for. He was even smart enough to have Joe keep his scales for him. He didn't have a large number of lighters or anything that could be used against him legally. He did keep pipes in the house, but only two, and they were hidden in the best hidden-compartment drawer I have ever seen. That drawer impressed me, and that was hard to do. No one walking into his house would know it was a drug house.

All the time I was in Washington, I was on the phone with Bryant constantly. Soon it became clear I was going to have to get back to Maui. I had been gone almost a month. I had to send Wilkes another doctor's note, and when I set out to forge it, I couldn't remember the name of the doctor I had used before. I also couldn't remember what type of cancer I had told everyone I had, cervical or ovarian, so I made up a new one to add to the mix. Lymphoma.

I knew it was only a matter of time before they figured it all out.

My last night with the dealer, I told him I was leaving in the morning. He was acting so possessive that I had no intention of getting back in touch with him. I was going to have to dump him and find a new supplier.

He barely let me go that night, and I was glad to get back to Carol's.

The next morning there were lots of calls from him on my cell phone. I sent them to voice mail, wanting to get rid of this guy as quickly as I could. Then the home phone rang and Carol told me it was for me.

I accepted the phone nervously, worried that it might be Bryant or my sergeant.

"Hi, Alli."

The dealer.

Shit, how had he gotten this number?

I was panicking but tried to play it cool.

"I just wanted to make sure you got what I left you," he said.

"Oh, what was that?" I asked.

Just then, my brother-in-law came in with flowers and a card.

"This was on the front steps. It's addressed to you, Alli," Tim said uncertainly.

"Yeah," I said on the phone. "It just arrived. I'll call you later."

"Who knows you're living here?" Tim asked.

"Well," I said, opening the card slowly. It was a homemade card, some sort of insane bullshit booklet about how much he loved me. How much he was going to miss me. How he would love me unconditionally. How he would love me forever. How—

I tried to shield it from Tim's eyes.

"It's this cop I've been working with in Everett," I said hurriedly. "That was him on the phone too. I knew he was a wack job, but apparently he's fallen in love with me." I tried to laugh it off as I continued manufacturing the lie—he was on the rebound, his girlfriend had jilted him unexpectedly, I'd helped him get over it by talking to him, and now he'd fallen in love with me, ha ha.

"It's kind of weird that he knows where we live," Tim said.

No shit. I had no idea how the dealer knew my sister's address. And phone number. I hadn't even told him I was staying with her. Had he followed me? Watched me? Was he doing surveillance on the house?

Fuck.

In a panic, I sent the dealer an email. I told him I was in law enforcement and that I couldn't see him anymore because of what I did for a living. I figured that would scare the shit out of him and he would never contact me again.

I was so wrong.

16

As soon as my flight landed in Maui, I turned on my phone. Four voice messages from the dealer, full of love and threat in equal measure.

When was I coming back, he wanted to know. He loved me more than anything on earth and needed me in his bed. We were soul mates and destined to be together. Every minute apart was torture.

Then: he knew I worked for MPD. He'd known since the beginning.

And by the way: he had a video of me smoking meth and having sex with him and he would send the video to MPD and Keawe if I didn't come back to Washington and see him that weekend.

How had he found out where I worked? How on earth did he know about Keawe?

Clearly, he had hacked into my email. I didn't believe him when he said he had a video, but that wasn't really important. How was I going to explain some drug dealer from Washington calling Keawe or MPD?

I was terrified. For the first time I saw that the career that I loved might not hold up against my using. Until now all I cared about was dope. Getting it, using it, doing whatever I had to to make sure I wasn't found out. Now I saw what I had done to my life.

Things were out of control. I was going to have to tell Keawe. MPD. Someone. I was going to have to get out of this web of lies.

Keawe called just as I walked in the door of my apartment. Part of me—a large part—wanted to break down and tell him everything. Instead, I sent his call to voice mail. I went into the bathroom, curled myself in a ball on the floor, and started to cry.

I lay there for a long, long time, aware that I was beginning to break down. The drug that had kept me going for so long, that had made me able to work harder and faster, was now working against me. The quantity I was consuming now, plus the potency of the dealer's meth, was too much for me. My brain was beginning to fail.

I recognized this.

And then.

And then, after finally understanding the gravity of the situation, after accepting for the first time what the drug had turned me into, I picked up a packet of meth instead of my phone. I ate the meth because you get higher faster that way. The taste is unbearable, but what addict cares about taste?

I decided to play along with the dealer. I would turn around and manipulate him just as much as he manipulated me. He was the only human being I knew who could give me what I wanted in the quantities I needed, and I was going to have to find a way to work around his craziness.

I sent him an email to tell him I would be there to see him on Friday, and I went in to work.

"Jesus, Alli," Wilkes said. "What are you doing back here? You need to take care of yourself."

"I am," I said. "I'm doing a lot better."

Wilkes looked unconvinced.

I didn't want to fuck up my cases, but I couldn't do the work.

All I could do in Maui was smoke. I kept thinking if I could just take one more hit I could sit down and finish the case.

I couldn't.

I lasted two weeks in Maui before I returned to Seattle. I was in such terrible shape when I left that I worried Wilkes or Roger Bryant would call my sister to see how I was doing, so when I got to her house, I set her phone to forward all incoming calls to my cell phone, knowing she wouldn't figure it out for a while.

I spent most of my time in Seattle with the dealer. He didn't mention MPD or the sex tape, just talked about how much in love with me he was. He was weird, but I settled into playing boyfriend and girlfriend with him. There were rules. I had to tell him how much I loved him all the time. I had to make him a drink exactly how he wanted it—a vodka with exactly five ice cubes. I couldn't wear a ponytail because he didn't like me in a ponytail.

There were rules all over the house, rules I was always learning. No shoes. Don't go in that bathroom, only this one. Don't go in the computer room unless I invite you. Don't go into the shop, ever. The spare room? Absolutely not.

It wasn't hard to follow the rules. I knew that was how I would keep getting my dope.

One day his friend Joe came over and sat at the table with the dealer. I was wandering around, starting little tweaker projects in the kitchen, ignoring the men until I saw Joe pull out a gun.

"Nice piece, huh, Alli?" he asked, laughing and waving it around, trying to intimidate me. I wasn't intimidated, but I was worried. I assumed Joe had no skills, and it was always the people who aren't trained that will shoot first.

The dealer had a gun too. He kept it in his shop for protection and took it out every now and again to clean it. I kept that in mind in case he ever got too crazy.

After another ten days in Seattle, I got ready to head back to Maui.

"I'd like that sex tape," I told the dealer casually, when I left. "So I can watch it while I'm away from you." It was the first time I had mentioned it.

"Sure," he said evenly. "I burned a DVD for you. As a gift. You can watch it and think about us."

"Oh thank you," I said. "It's so thoughtful of you to do that."

I knew he wasn't stupid enough to give me his only copy of the tape, but I thought if I acted like it didn't matter that he had made it, he wouldn't do anything as stupid as calling MPD.

When I got back to Maui, I watched the DVD. It was pretty damning. I didn't care about the sex part, but anyone who watched it would see me smoking meth and I would be busted.

I hid the tape in my apartment, in an old purse on my closet shelf.

I stayed in Maui for a week trying to work, but no matter how long I stayed at the station, no matter how much dope I smoked, I couldn't concentrate enough to finish a report everyone was waiting for. When Wilkes took a look at what I was doing, he frowned and said, "Jesus, Alli. Maybe you're too sick to work."

"I'm not," I said, but started taking more days off. As soon as I realized I couldn't get anything done, I headed back to Seattle.

This became my pattern: stay in Maui until I couldn't stand

it, then go back to Seattle and see the dealer for more drugs. It went on like this for a long time—weeks turning into a month and then two. I told the department I was returning to the mainland for treatment, and they believed me, even though I looked sicker and sicker. My meth use was massive, and after a while we started adding heroin to the mix.

When I was in Seattle, I had to be on the phone a lot with MPD, and that never made the dealer happy. One time the dealer found me talking to Keawe and got really pissed. When I got off the phone, I asked him for some dope, and he said, "Why don't you get dope from Keawe if he loves you so much?"

"Come on," I said, ignoring his comment about Keawe. "I need a hit."

"I don't have any for you right now," he said. "You have to wait." He turned and walked away from me, and I followed him into the kitchen.

"Don't be a dick," I said. "I haven't had any all day and you gave me that heroin last night. I need meth to come down from that."

Suddenly he turned and said, "Don't tell me what you need, you bitch."

"Don't be such an asshole." I pushed him with two hands, and suddenly we were in a pushing and shoving fight that only ended when he slammed my hip into the kitchen counter.

"Quit it!" I said, rubbing my hip.

He turned and walked away. That shove gave me a nasty bruise on my right hip bone, but I didn't think any more about it. I brushed it off as the heroin and us getting too high.

He brought me a bowl of dope a few minutes later, and he started giving me more heroin that night as well. Soon everything was back to normal.

• • •

When I got back to Maui a few days later, I found Keawe waiting for me at my apartment. I was happy to see him. Fucked up as I was, he always made me feel things were going to be okay.

"What are you doing here?" I asked.

"Listen, Alli," he said, "while you were away Erin and I moved some of your stuff to her house."

"What stuff?" I asked suspiciously.

"Your clothes, your uniform, your toiletries and such."

I felt confused. I had counted on having a hit as soon as I walked in the door, and I was so focused on it that I couldn't really understand what he was saying.

"You went through my things?" I asked. *This was it*, I thought. He'd found a pipe—he was going to tell me he knew about the ice. Or he'd found the sex tape, or the dealer's name and address, or—

But I had been so careful about hiding things. Maybe he hadn't found anything.

"We just want to help," Keawe said. "Erin can look after you at her house."

"I'm not going," I said. I was pissed that they'd done this without asking, as if I were a child. "Bring my stuff back," I demanded.

"Look at you," he said gently. "You look like shit, you weigh about eighty pounds—"

"A hundred and sixteen," I said, then, "Excuse me," and ran for the bathroom. I just about made it before I started throwing up.

Keawe was right behind me. He placed his warm hand on the small of my back and gathered my matted hair away from the sides of the toilet. "See?" he said. "There's no way you can stay by yourself. You need someone to take care of you, and I can't be there all the time."

"It's just, it's just—" was all I got out before I started heaving again.

"I know," he said. "It's the chemo."

No, I thought, *it's the heroin withdrawal.*

And then, *Oh shit, what am I going to do now?*

17

My friendship with Erin had continued to be mostly one-sided. She would call me and I wouldn't call her. She would invite me places and I wouldn't go. She would buy me gifts and I would get her nothing.

Erin wanted to be girlfriends, and I wanted to operate solo, but she had been persistent and eventually I had come around. Even though I hid all my secrets from her, she was probably my closest female friend on Maui. Now she wanted to take care of me.

Because I had stopped using heroin so abruptly, I went straight into withdrawal. I was throwing up six or eight times a day at Erin's, and I had the fevers, shakes, and diarrhea, all of which only helped my cancer story.

As soon as I moved into Erin's house, Keawe said, "Let me get you some weed to help with the nausea." So I would go in the bathroom, pretending to smoke marijuana for my chemo and smoke the meth instead. Neither Keawe nor Erin had any idea what was going on. Erin was an easy friend for me to have because like many cops she drank too much, and most nights, she would fall soundly asleep on the couch and not even realize I was up.

So much for taking care of me.

I was fine with that.

Erin lived in a new subdivision nicknamed Coptown because so much of MPD lived there. It was easy for my colleagues from work to come by her house to see me, and they did—all the time. "We love you, Alli," they would say. "You're going to make it through, you're going to be okay." Some of them brought flowers.

When Wilkes came, he had news for me. He said, "Alli, you know we want you to get better, and we need you to take as much time as you need. But your sick leave's run out."

"Am I being placed on suspension?" I asked. "Because I understand—"

"No, we're not going to suspend you. One of the officers has donated his sick leave."

"No," I said. "I don't want anyone to do that. Who was it?"

"I can't tell you that, but I will tell you that once everyone heard, they did the same thing. Eventually I sent out a memo, and you wouldn't believe the response."

"Oh God," I said. "No." I continued protesting, but Wilkes held up his hand like a stop sign.

"You can always count on your brothers in blue," he said.

I turned my face away, so ashamed at what my lies had led to. Jesus, I had to put an end to this. I needed to say, *Stop, call it all off, I don't really have cancer.*

But I couldn't.

These wonderful friends, these wonderful colleagues—they

just wanted to help in a helpless situation. Even though I couldn't eat, they kept bringing me food. They would have done anything to help.

The next afternoon, the chief of police came by with a casserole his wife had made. I just wanted to die.

People were so shocked when they saw me. Because I was on ice I had no idea how bad I looked. I was down to 115 pounds, hadn't brushed my hair in six or seven days, and was vomiting all the time. I thought I looked amazing.

After the heroin withdrawals, my body was so tired that it didn't matter how much meth I smoked. I slept. I slept for forty-eight hours and that made Erin think I was even sicker.

"I have a plan," she told me one day. "My mom and I are organizing a fund-raiser."

"A fund-raiser?" I asked.

"Yeah. To help you pay for your treatment. I know everyone's been donating their sick leave and that helps, but you still have all those bills to pay."

"Erin, I don't want you to do that," I said. "I have insurance. I don't need—"

"It's already in the works," she said. "We're going to have a dinner and a silent auction at one of the Kaanapali hotels. You know everyone will come. We're going to . . ." As she told me about the plans, my heart sank even further.

A fund-raiser? A fucking silent auction for a lying, law-breaking, whore drug addict?

Like so many times before, I wanted to die. Looking the people I loved in the eye and lying to them remains the most painful part of my story.

It took ten or eleven days for me to get through the withdrawal and the crash, and after that I couldn't handle people coming by the house anymore. I couldn't handle the lies. By that point, more than eighty fellow cops had donated their sick leave to me.

I had to go. I had to get out of there. The dealer in Washington was expecting me, but I couldn't face him. I told Keawe and Erin I needed to go to Los Angeles to see a new doctor, try a new cancer treatment. Keawe didn't want to let me go, but I insisted this was the best doctor in the country. If he could have, Keawe would have come with me, and then I would have been screwed. It was one of the few times in our relationship that I was glad he was a married man.

I flew to Los Angeles just as I said I was going to—and then, with my last remaining cash, I bought a one-way ticket to New Mexico to see my mom. I suppose I thought there was some way she would be able to fix everything for me.

My mom had no idea I was coming. I called her from the airport and she had to leave work early to come pick me up.

As soon as she saw me, she knew I was sick. "Alli, what's happened?" she asked me. Hugging me, she made me feel protected, okay. She took me home, and it was so good to be safe in my own house, with my family, that I crashed for twenty-four hours straight.

When I woke up, she said, "I'm taking you to the emergency room."

"No," I said. "I'm fine now. I just needed to get some sleep."

I knew I couldn't go to the ER. Any doctor would take one look at me and say, *This girl's not sick, she's high.*

"You're sick, Alli. Look at you."

"Why do you always tell me how horrible I look?" I yelled at her. "I'm *tired*. I'm working too hard. Just let me rest. Isn't that what you're supposed to do when you come home?"

My mom winced. She could see in my eyes that I was going to run, and she was trying to find a way to contain me.

"Okay," she relented. "We don't need to go to the ER, but I'll make an appointment with Dr. Warren. She's known you your whole life."

"Fine," I said, knowing I would leave before going to any appointment.

I spent a week with my mom, sleeping and getting high. She had a new dog, a mastiff named Bella that she had rescued from a shelter. She had gotten Bella with me in mind and had started the paperwork to send her to Maui to be with me. Mo had been a special dog, but so was Bella, and I liked her immediately. I spent a lot of time cuddling her that week.

The day before the doctor's appointment my mom had scheduled, my mom and I got in a big fight. I knew I couldn't go to the doctor, but my mom wouldn't let it go. I finally had to resort to a new lie.

"Look," I said. "Okay, I have been sick. I just didn't want you to worry."

"What do you have?" she asked.

"I'm on sick leave from the department. It's a blood disorder, but I'm almost cured now. When I get back to Maui, I'll definitely see my doctor. I promise. I don't want to go to the ER here. They'll just run a bunch of expensive tests and start from scratch."

"What sort of blood disorder?" my mom asked. "Is it serious? Are you—"

"My spleen hasn't been functioning. I'm on antibiotics. I just need to get back."

"I don't want to put you on a plane in that condition," my mom said. "You're not making any sense. We'll see Dr. Warren tomorrow afternoon. She knows us. She won't—"

"No!" I shouted at her. "There's *no time*. I have to go. MPD is expecting me tomorrow morning for a deposition. I've got to be there."

"Something's really wrong, Alli," my mom said. "I know you. I can tell." And then, for the first time in a year and a half, someone asked me the right question: "Are you on drugs?"

I looked at my mom. I was a pro at making up lies on demand. Usually I started talking before I even knew what I was going to say, but my mom's question stunned me. I hesitated for a second, and then I felt pissed. Pissed that I'd given my mom enough evidence to ask such a question.

I yanked up my sleeves and showed her my arms. "Do you see tracks, Mom? Do you?"

"Alli . . . ," she said slowly.

"No tracks. Why would I be on drugs?"

I could tell she thought my reaction was strange. She was debating what to say, how to handle me.

"I'm going now," I said. "Either you drive me to the airport, or I'm calling a cab." As if I had enough money for a cab.

"What time's your flight?"

"I don't have a ticket yet," I said.

"Well then, let's get you a ticket." This seemed to cheer my mom up a little. Here was a way she could actually help. She could get me a ticket.

"I'll buy your ticket," she said. "We can book it online."

"No, I'll get it at the airport. It would be better if you just gave me cash." I still didn't know where I was going, but I knew I would need cash for dope.

She drove me to the airport and tried to come in with me. "I have an idea," she said. "I'll fly with you as far as California. Just to make sure you're okay."

"That's ridiculous," I said. "I need to get to Maui. If I waste any more time, there will be a warrant out for me. I have to go."

"Honey, call me the minute you get there. The very minute."

"Okay," I said.

"I love you," she said.

She gave me a big hug and a wad of cash.

I walked away.

I didn't look back.

As I waited for the plane, I started to formulate a plan.

I would go back to Maui to die. My plan was to eat my gun.

My firearms were at Erin's, and I didn't want to kill myself there. I didn't want her to have to deal with that mess, all the guilt. I was going to have to get my gun out of Erin's without her seeing me. I didn't want to see her. Or Keawe. Or anyone. I just wanted to die.

My plan was hazy.

I got as far as LA. I had less than a gram of meth with me, not nearly enough to make me comfortable enough to pull the trigger. At this point I was using almost an eight ball a day, and I didn't have enough cash to buy more meth.

I was out of options. I couldn't go to Maui and face all my lies. I couldn't go back to New Mexico and be hauled off to the ER.

By cruel process of elimination, the only safe place for me was with the dealer in Seattle.

It seems absurd to me now that I felt I couldn't stay with my mother who loved me or go home to Keawe, Erin, and all my friends in Maui. These people would have done anything for me. Anything. They would have gotten me help instantly. They would have forgiven me. And yet in my warped addict's mind, I saw Seattle and the crazy, threatening, blackmailing dealer as my only refuge.

I called the dealer and he bought me a one-way ticket from LA to Washington.

It would be eight months before I saw Maui again, and when I did I would be in handcuffs.

18

The dealer picked me up at the airport. I found him waiting at the curb, leaning against his red truck, holding flowers. *Flowers.* Just like Keawe did, I thought, and then dismissed that thought. He was nothing like Keawe.

"I've missed you so much," I said, lying, hugging him, smelling the flowers, trying to smile. This was the part I would have to continue to play—his girlfriend, in love with him—in order to get my dope. I chattered on. "I missed you! I'm so glad to see you because I really, really missed you."

"I knew you'd be back," he said, taking my bag and throwing it in the back of the truck. It was a tiny overnight bag. When I left Maui, I had packed only for a weekend in Albuquerque, just an extra pair of jeans and a couple of tank tops.

"You get the ticket all right?" he asked.

"Hey, thanks so much for sending it," I said. "I'll pay you back,

I promise." He made no response to this. I knew I would be paying for it one way or another.

I continued on. "I'm just a little short of cash right now. I'll get the money to you, though. You know I'm good for it. I just got to the airport and couldn't find my credit card. I know it's here somewhere." I was meth-talking, running on and on about pointless things. And lying: I was flat broke.

The inside of his truck reeked of cigarettes. I was happy to try any drug in the world, but I had never really smoked, and the smell of tobacco made me nauseous. I was sure he had dope hidden in the truck somewhere, but no one without a dope dog would be able to find it.

How long would he make me wait before giving me dope? Probably just until I slept with him.

I curled up in the front seat, my feet on the dash. I needed a hit.

"You should put your feet on the floor," he said. I looked down at my feet. All I had on were the flip-flops I had left Maui with. I wished I had brought my sneakers with me. It was much colder in Seattle than in Albuquerque.

I slid my feet down to the floor.

"You should wash your feet," he said.

I nodded, trying to stare ahead, but instead my eyes darted from the road to the mirrors to him to my feet to my bag. When I looked at him, his expression was stern. He had one of those faces that looked threatening except when he smiled, and he almost never smiled. His bald head, his thick neck, the heavy silver chain he wore around it—almost like a bicycle chain—all these things made him look just as tough as he wanted people to think he was.

I put my bag on my lap and started sorting through everything in it. My bag was my latest tweaker thing. Twenty or thirty times a day I checked to make sure everything was there—my badge, my phone, my wallet (empty), my ID, the hairbrush I never used, my keys, a collection of empty Tic Tac boxes.

We didn't speak the rest of the drive, but when we pulled into his driveway the dealer said again, "You should wash your feet."

"Okay, sure. They got dirty in my flip-flops, but I can take care of them right away. Sure. I can definitely do that."

I got out of the car and walked quickly toward the house.

I instinctively glanced upward as I reached the porch. He kept two security cameras in the front of the house so he could monitor comings and goings.

Inside, the house was cool and dark. He always kept it cool, the drapes always drawn. No one could look in, no one could look out.

I took off my flip-flops and left them at the door. No shoes allowed was the rule. The tile floor felt cold on my feet.

"Let's go upstairs," I said. Instinctively, I looked for the cat, which always made itself scarce, hiding. It was nowhere to be seen.

The sooner we fucked, the sooner I would earn my dope. I didn't have a plan beyond that. I couldn't think about Maui and Keawe and MPD, or Albuquerque and my family. I had been holding these worlds together with my lies for so long, I must have known they were about to crash down around me. This house was the only place where I could be who I really was.

I had turned toward the staircase and was putting one foot on the bottom stair when I felt something slam into the small of my back. It felt like an explosion and I fell forward onto the stairs. Before I could even turn around I felt fists pounding me, this time on the upper back.

"I bet you wash your fucking feet for Keawe," he said. "You think you can get in my bed with filthy feet like that?"

I managed to twist around and spring to my feet. I was a cop; I wasn't going to let someone get away with hitting me. I landed a punch on his jaw and kicked him in the kneecap, then tried to get him in a choke hold. I almost had him, too, but he was so much bigger and stronger—he had the build of a Tongan, and I had never been able to arrest a Tongan without his cooperation.

It was nothing for him to shake me off.

"What are you doing?" I yelled. "I didn't mean anything." I couldn't believe what was happening. We had had pushing and shoving fights before, but I had dismissed those as junkie fights, times when we had just gotten too high.

"I'll wash my damned feet," I yelled. "Don't be an asshole!"

"You will never get into my bed with feet like that," he said. "Do you understand?"

He pulled me up by one arm like a doll or a small child and led me upstairs to the bathroom, where I sat on the side of the tub scrubbing my feet and crying. When I was done, I tiptoed into the hallway.

"This is for you," he said, handing me an ice pipe, pulling me into the bedroom. "It's really good dope."

I grabbed it from him, inhaled as much as I could get into my lungs. He took a hit himself and gave the pipe back to me.

"I'm not a bad guy, Alli," he said, starting to stroke my hair. "I'm not perfect, but I'm not a bad guy." He pulled me closer to him and put his arms around me. "I want you to remember something I told you the last time you were here. I love you very much. I love you *unconditionally*. You understand?"

I nodded.

"That means that I will love you no matter what you do. A lot of people wouldn't understand how I can forgive you for what you've done, but I can."

I nodded again—pretending that I knew what he was talking about—and he started to take off my clothes. My skin was red, but there was no bruising yet. He hadn't hit me in the face or the arms. Even in his rage, he had that much control. There would be no outward signs of a beating.

I settled into a great high as we started to have sex.

I would like to say that after he fell asleep I ran for the door, got help, and got away, but nothing like that happened. I look back on that first fight and find that, like so many times during my using, there was the right path, the clear path, the path any sane person would have taken, and the other path, the addict's path, the wrong one. I chose the wrong path every time. Every single fucking time.

Why didn't I leave that first time he hit me? It didn't make any sense. Later I replayed the actions of my addict self like someone watching a horror film and yelling, *Don't go into the house! Don't go into the house*, I wanted to scream. *Get the hell out!*

He slept for a couple of hours. I didn't. I had at least another week before I would crash again. He had left some dope next to the table so I kept smoking, and when he woke up he joined me. We smoked again, had sex again, and then he said, "I want to do something special for you."

He put down a line of meth and then heated up a glass tube, thin as a straw and so hot that he had to hold it with pliers.

"Here you go," he said. "Hot line. The best high of your life." I inhaled the line of meth through the tube and it went up my nose just as it turned from solid to gas. Of course it burned because it was so hot, but it eliminated that step when you're smoking when the smoke travels from the glass bowl up the pipe to your mouth. The meth felt strong and completely pure, like it was altering the chemical composition of my body. If I were a normal person, it

would probably have given me a heart attack; instead, I felt an explosion of euphoria.

"Oh my God," I said. "It feels so good. This is just so great. Oh
my God. Oh my God."

"I knew you'd like it," he said. "I planned it for you."

I practically forgot that he had hit me. The ice was so great and
he was letting me have as much as I wanted.

After a while he had to go work at his fake specialty carpentry
job, and he took me with him. He had built a gazebo in somebody's
backyard, and he wanted me to help him paint it. I liked the painting. I was so high it felt exciting to me. I kept smelling the smooth
white paint, kept watching it drop from the brush after I dunked it
into the can. He had to keep reminding me to paint.

A young woman with a baby in her arms came out from the
big brick house to talk to him. She didn't say anything to me,
but I could see the puzzlement in her eyes. Why was there a girl
in flip-flops and a tank top, clearly freezing in the cloudy Seattle summer, painting her gazebo? She was probably two or three
years older than I was, married to a techie wizard, getting a gazebo
built behind her mansion, and I was a meth-addicted vice cop
who hadn't showered in days and had just had the shit kicked out
of her by a drug dealer.

I didn't know what she was thinking about me, but all I felt for
her was pity: *You have no idea what you're missing. You have no idea
how fucking great this is.*

Over the next few days, my bruises ripened to red, dark blue, black.
They hurt like hell and then started to heal. The dealer bought me
a couple of new tank tops. I honestly thought things were going to

be okay. Sure, he had freaked out when I first got there, but it was just because he was so jealous of Keawe. Now he couldn't have been nicer.

When I was first on patrol, I never understood why a woman wouldn't leave someone who hit her, and why she would keep her children in that situation. So many times when I had responded to a domestic abuse call and was trying to cuff the husband or boyfriend, the woman who had called 911 for help—the woman he had hit—would come at me with a blunt object. "Don't arrest him, you *haole* bitch!" she would yell. Once a cop was there actually arresting the guy, she couldn't go through with it, and the excuses started to flow.

He didn't mean it.

He's had too much to drink.

He's too high.

His work is so stressful.

The kids are driving him crazy.

Whatever these women said, they always had a reason to defend their men, and it always pissed me off. I wasn't showing them a hell of a lot of compassion, so my lieutenant sent me to a domestic violence class where I learned about the cycle of abuse. And now, with all my training, with my years as a cop, I was trapped in that same vicious cycle. I had been a "pounder" in vice—all my cases recovered more than a pound of narcotics—and I had been considered a badass. Now I had let this guy beat the crap out of me just so I could get more dope.

I tried to keep myself from thinking about MPD, but Keawe was on my mind always. I knew when I didn't turn up when I was supposed to, Keawe would worry, and sure enough, every time I turned on my cell there was a message from him. My mom was used to not hearing from me for weeks at a time—I would tell her I had an undercover job and she would leave me alone—but Keawe was a problem. His messages sounded increasingly urgent. He seemed to think I had gone somewhere to die. As time passed—and I had no idea how much, a day, three days, a week—I started to miss him terribly. Once, when the dealer was safely working in his shop and I was upstairs folding his laundry, I called Keawe.

"Alli!" he said. "I've been so worried about you. Why haven't you returned my messages? Where are you?"

Hearing his voice, I started to cry.

"I'm sorry," I said. "It's just that I'm so weak. I wanted to tell you I miss you. And I love you."

"Everyone's looking for you. We were expecting you on Tuesday. Where are you?"

I couldn't take the questions, the concerns. All I wanted was the voice.

"I can't talk," I said. "Please, just tell me—do you love me?"

"Of course I love you, babe. Everything's going to be okay. Come see me and we'll talk about things. Are you on your way back?"

I started to feel dizzy and sat on the bed next to the folded clothes. Fuck—what was I going to say to him? I babbled on about my feelings, how he was the only one for me, how I loved him more than life, saying all the same things I told the dealer, only meaning them.

"When are you coming back?" he repeated.

"I'm in LA," I said. "I'm in a hospice and I don't think I'll be able to see you again." I could hear how hollow my lies sounded, but Keawe didn't seem to notice. I knew I could never go back to Maui, never face my friends and colleagues and their donated sick days and their fund-raisers.

I didn't listen for his answer. I turned my cell phone off abruptly so I wouldn't hear him call back, then put it in my purse under the bed.

A little while later, the dealer appeared in the doorway.

"You done with the laundry?" he asked.

"Yeah, I just finished."

"Let me see."

I pointed to the folded clothes on the bed. "I could really use a hit," I said.

He walked from the doorway to the bed in one long stride and picked up a pair of his boxer shorts. "What the hell is this?"

I tried not to laugh. "Your underwear?"

"You think I'm going to wear these?" he asked. "You think I'm going to wear them without them being ironed?"

"I didn't know," I said. "You didn't say anything about—"

I saw the look in his eyes.

I knew what was coming.

I ran for the stairs, but he was right behind me, and as soon as I made it down, he was able to grab me by the hair. Holding my hair, he pounded my ribs. "You little whore!"

I fought back as hard as I could, but I couldn't get away. He kept throwing blows at my breasts, my stomach, my ribs. I pushed and kicked and bit as viciously as I could.

He kicked me in the stomach, and I fell to the ground at the foot of the stairs, trying to breathe. He flipped me over onto my stomach. "Open your mouth," he barked.

I had no idea what he was going to do.

When I opened my mouth, he pushed my face down so hard that I was biting the corner of the stair. What he did next—

Oh God, some things I just can't find the words for. As I bit the step, he brought his foot down on the back of my head. I could feel the corner of my lips cracking. *This is it*, I thought, *he's going to kill me. He's going to break my neck.*

I didn't say anything. I couldn't.

He pushed his foot down harder on my head until I felt I would pass out. As all air to my lungs was cut off, I made a gurgling, choking noise that seemed to satisfy him and he took his foot away. Gasping for air, I brought my hand to my mouth, expecting to find my mouth torn open.

I knew heading for the door right away was the wrong thing to do. I wasn't sure I could outrun him in bare feet, and even if I could, I didn't know the area well, didn't even know where to run. Would the neighbors help me? Would they call the cops for me? Even if they did, would the cops believe me, or just think we were two junkies fighting, so there was no need to arrest anyone here?

Mostly, as I lay spread out on the stairs, weeping, trying to figure out what to do, I was just pissed that he had won. I had been in so many fights as a cop, but I had always come out on top. The meth had now weakened me to the point of near defenselessness.

"He doesn't love you, you know," the dealer said calmly.

"Who?" I asked.

"If he loved you, he'd be with you. But who's with you? Me. I'm the one who loves you."

Keawe. He knew I had talked to Keawe. But how? He never could have heard from downstairs.

I thought of the security cameras in the front of the house, all the colored lightbulbs in his shop. I had brushed these off as his weird tweaker projects, but what if he was filming me, recording me?

Maybe there were cameras, hidden cameras. Wildly, my eyes

roamed around, but then he was there and we were hotlining—pure rich meth, the meth I had always wanted.

I stopped looking for cameras, for tape recorders, for anything, and I thought, *This is okay. He knows all the shit I've done, he knows about the cancer lies and being a dirty cop. Wow, he must really love me if he's going to stay with me after knowing all that.*

A beating now and then's not so bad.

19

Once I began to suspect there were cameras in the house, I started to keep track of the dealer's movements at all times. He would never really let me in the computer room—he had three computers, plus a monitor for the outside security cameras—and I knew there was something in that room that he didn't want me to see. He always turned on the screen saver before he let me in the room.

I began to notice him going into the closet off the third bedroom all the time, and when I asked about it, he told me it led to the attic above the shop where he was doing some repairs. Some days the cat would follow him, and once he came down muttering, "Shit! Damn cat had kittens up there."

The next day, when he was in the shop, I crept into the attic. I didn't see the kittens, but I did see cables everywhere, many more than you would need for cable TV. Once I saw them, I guessed what they were, but to be sure I followed one of the cables through the attic floor. After pacing it out, I went downstairs to see that it led to a camera in the recessed light above the living room.

I went upstairs to the bedroom and checked the recessed lighting there. Another camera: that must have been how he made the sex tape. He was filming everything.

Everything.

I charged into the shop. "What the hell are you doing with all those cameras?" I asked him.

"So what?" he said, not even looking up from his worktable.

"I need my privacy."

"What kind of privacy does a whore like you need?" he asks.

"I am not a whore!"

"The hell you aren't," he said. "I'm spending all my money supporting you. I can't even make my truck payments this month, you're costing me so much money."

I knew this wasn't true. He wasn't having money problems—he made plenty from his carpentry and a ton from dealing. Plus he ran a couple of Home Depot scams that I didn't really understand. I had seen him with wads of cash.

"You need to earn your rent," he said. "You're going to have to start earning it."

"Oh yeah? I think I already *am* earning it."

His eyes went almost entirely black. I could feel his rage. But instead of attacking me he started laughing.

His laughter was terrifying.

I ran for the stairs. He pushed me from behind. On the ground, I started crawling and made it to the top of the stairway when he kicked me in the stomach. Falling from my hands and knees onto my back, I tried to breathe. He had knocked the wind out of me.

He grabbed me by the hair and began to drag me while I struggled to breathe.

Suddenly he let go of me and in the calmest, most terrifying voice he said, "Catch your breath, honey. I'm sorry."

I caught my breath, probably within a few seconds, and I thought the fight was over, but when I tried to sit up, he grabbed me by the hair once again. He was trying to drag me into the bedroom, but I grabbed the railing on the stairs. He hit me in the ear and then let go. Using both hands now, he continued dragging me by the hair. I could hear the hair ripping out, almost like a rubber band snapping.

He screamed, "Earning it? You worthless cunt, you're not earning anything."

I was so furious I don't remember feeling any pain at that moment. I just wanted to get away.

I grabbed his wrists behind my head. I was kicking and screaming to make him stop, but he kept dragging me, all the way to the bed, where he finally let go. I lay on my side on the floor, looking at him. Strands of my ripped out hair were caught in his fingers. He took that hair and shoved it in my mouth.

I tried to spit the ripped-out strands out of my mouth.

"Don't you spit at me!" he screamed. He grabbed me by the throat and threw me on the bed but my legs were hanging over the edge. He was trying to pull my jeans off and couldn't get the button. Enraged, he yanked my jeans straight down. At this point I stopped fighting. I was only crying.

Once my jeans were down, he turned me over and pushed my face into the comforter. He started to rape me anally. I screamed from the pain. Finally he stopped and got off me. It hurt to breathe at this point.

"Just kill me!" I screamed. "You hate me so much, just kill me."

He left the room, and I heard the shower running. I assumed he was getting into the shower, and I didn't move. "Kill me now!" I yelled after him. "I want to die. All I want is to die."

Bent over the bed partway, with half my weight on my kneeling legs, I still felt too weak to support myself.

I slid down to the floor, and when he came back into the room he brushed the hair out of my face.

"Get away from me," I said. "Just get away."

"You need to get in the shower," he said.

"I can't. I can't get up."

"Get up. I don't want blood and shit on the carpet."

"I can't," I said weakly.

He picked me up in the gentlest way and carried me to the shower.

"It's okay," he said. "It's okay, I still love you."

He set me down in the shower. He was a different man now. My caregiver.

I felt wetness and realized I was bleeding anally. I didn't know how much, but it scared me. And I hurt. I could barely stand the water hitting my backside, so I stood up. He got in the shower with me and washed me and hugged me until I stopped shaking.

"You're okay," he said. "You're okay."

"The water stings," I said. "I want to get out."

"Let's get you cleaned up first," he said. He washed my hair and massaged my head.

"I've got a headache," I said. "I'm going to throw up."

He took me out of the shower and started drying me off gently. I don't know what this says about me, but the next thing I said to him was this: "I love you, and I'm sorry."

He hugged me. "I'm sorry too. Do you want to lay down?"

"No. I don't want to move at all."

"Get dressed then." He picked up my jeans then and said, "Good thing you didn't get blood on your jeans. It's your only pair."

He disappeared then, and I got dressed. It took me a long time to pull my jeans up. I could hear him calling me from the computer room. I put my shirt on carefully. Every movement felt like I was still ripping.

I walked slowly down the hall to the computer room, where I was rarely allowed to go. This time, he invited me in.

"Sit down," he said. Porn was playing on his computer screen. He was sitting there naked in front of it. He loaded a bowl and we smoked a lot of meth.

He continued watching the porn and pointed out what he liked about the girls on the screen. I let my eyes wander around the room, trying to figure out how the cameras were connected to the computer.

Later I found all the footage, organized in different files on his main computer. He was very particular. Most of the files were names of women; some were just dates. I didn't have time to look at all of them, but I found all the footage of me. It was more than disturbing, how much he liked to watch, what he liked to watch. He had sound clips of me, phone conversations I had with Keawe, everything. I found another file he kept on me, emails from work, emails between Keawe and me. He had all the contacts from my phone. My mom's address. All my sister's information. He also had my father's phone number, which I didn't even have.

He had investigated me more than I had ever investigated any of my targets. On his computer I found a file called "vice." I tried to open it, but it was password protected. I hated to think what was in that file.

Later I would find all this, but for now we were back to playing boyfriend and girlfriend. Only the girlfriend had just been raped, and every single movement she made was recorded, broadcast, re-played, and saved in this very room.

20

It took days for that pain to go away. Not only did my ass hurt, my back stung from rug burns I had gotten while he dragged me across the floor. The dealer gave me painkillers—oxys—to help. This was the worst it had been, though it would get worse. Worse not because the beatings got worse, though they did. It was the feeling that I might not survive. Every day I thought about suicide, but eventually I realized I might not be the one to take my life. He might kill me first.

I don't have one simple answer when it comes to why I didn't try to get away after that. Ask for help. A neighbor. Anyone. After a while, I knew that calling the cops was out of the question. He was so careful not to leave bruises on me. His ex-wife had filed a restraining order against him, and he didn't want to draw any attention to himself. Just as he hid his drugs and paraphernalia, he also hid his abuse of me. I knew from my experience as a cop that there would be no way for me to prove what he had done. Once I found the film footage on his computer, he encrypted it.

Stripped of my sense of self, unable to move or think without questioning the outcome, I quietly resigned myself to the idea that being with him—trapped in that house—was my fate. Nothing else really existed. The idea of dreams or any sort of future was shut out. I lived day to day, sometimes minute to minute. He had a way of igniting meth-induced rage within me while also beating me into submission. It got to the point where I wouldn't dare touch him for fear of the consequences. I was breaking physically and already broken emotionally.

Over time, I figured out the details of his camera system. He had them hidden in every room—even the bathrooms, especially the bathrooms—so he always knew where I went. If I went from one room to another, a colored light in his shop would alert him. If I opened the front door, he would get a text message on his cell phone. His tweaker thing was technology—microphones, cameras, sensors—and for an addict, he was brilliant.

I was a virtual prisoner in that house, watched all the time. If he left the house to work or do a deal, he would bring in Tiffany or one of his drug groupies to babysit me.

Around this time, the dealer moved the kittens from the attic into the guest bedroom on the second floor, just at the top of the stairs. Of course I begged him to let me have a kitten, but once he knew I wanted one, he used that against me.

I don't remember at what point he started abusing them to get to me, but he locked the kittens inside the room and kept the mother out. He let all the kittens cry while the mom went crazy outside the door.

"Would you let her in?" I screamed at him. "Please let her in."

"Goddamned cats," was all he would say.

I only saw the kittens once or twice and was not allowed to hold or touch them. He didn't hold them either, and separated from their mother, with no human interaction and very little food, they soon became feral. They never stopped crying. They made horrible sounds. I had never had an experience with feral cats before, but they were vicious. I could hear them clawing at the rug, the wall, the door. Eventually the entire stairway began to smell from all the feces in the room. I became terrified of that room, and of those cats. Day and night, their screaming tormented me.

Many times afterward, I tried to go back and reconstruct the timeline of my life in that house. How long was I there? How many days or weeks or months? How much time passed between beatings?

I didn't know. I could sometimes remember on what day of the week something occurred—a Tuesday, for example, definitely a Tuesday—but had no idea which Tuesday, in which month, even in which year. The dealer kept me so high that I barely knew where I was most of the time. I knew time was passing in that house but I had no idea how much.

Nor did I know that everyone was looking for me.

When I didn't show up in Maui as expected, the department started to worry. Keawe became suspicious after our phone conversation and believed something was very wrong.

Thinking that my mother and father were dead, Keawe tracked down my sister. By this point, Carol had realized she wasn't getting any phone calls and had reset the call forwarding on her phone. Keawe's call went right to her.

"This is Officer Davis," Keawe told Carol. "One of Alli's beat partners. I'm worried about her. We were expecting her in Maui five days ago and she didn't show."

"She didn't?" Carol asked. "I haven't talked to her, but I know she got on a plane to Maui a few days ago."

"I spoke to her briefly," Keawe said, "but she didn't sound good, and she won't return any of my messages. I know she's in LA, but I don't know where."

"LA? What in the world is she doing there? Have you talked to my mom yet?"

"Your mom?" Keawe asked, uncertainly.

"Yes. Our mom."

"Alli told me your mother was dead."

"What?"

Carol didn't waste time on the phone with Keawe. She immediately called my mom, and the two began a frantic search, calling and emailing everyone they could think of who might know where I was. Carol was still in occasional contact with our father, and she emailed him and his wife, Claire, in Florida. Claire did a Google search and came across an online flyer advertising one of the fund-raisers Erin had organized to raise money for my cancer treatment. Claire emailed the flyer to my sister with two words: "What's up?"

Panicked, Carol called Keawe. "How could you keep this horrific secret from us?" she demanded. "How could you not have enough respect to alert the family to this nightmare?"

Keawe was shocked that the family didn't know about my cancer.

"How could she not tell you?" he said. "She has stage four ovarian cancer. And lymphoma."

"Are you sure?" Carol asked.

"Of course. She's very ill. Too ill to travel very far."

At the dealer's house, I hadn't been answering calls, but I did listen to my messages sometimes, just to hear my family's and friends' voices. After she spoke to Keawe, Carol left me a message.

"What is going on, Alli?" the message said. "You have cancer! I'm so scared that you're alone and hurting. We're devastated, and we love you. You need to talk to us. Please. Call me as soon as you get this message. We need to hear from you." At the end, her voice broke, and she whispered, "God, do you really have cancer?"

I didn't call Carol back, but I did manage to call my mom.

"Alli!" she said. "Thank God. We can't believe what we're hearing. Cancer?"

"That's right," I said. "I do have cancer. I just don't want anyone to see me like this. I've got lymphoma." I explained to her that I was in a hospice in LA and was expecting to die soon.

My mom began sobbing and tried to ask me a hundred questions. Down the hall, the cats wailed and hissed.

"I've got to go," I said. "I'm sorry. I love you all." I hung up the phone.

I had nothing to say to my mom. I *did* feel like I was dying, not from cancer, but from meth. I had already accepted that I would never see my family again. I just didn't want them to know what had become of me. My crazy meth brain convinced me that my mother would buy this, would understand I was about to die and quietly leave the matter alone. That's how worthless I felt. I sat on the carpeted floor next to the bed and listened to myself cry almost as loudly as the cats.

Carol and my mom began calling cancer hospitals in LA but no one acknowledged having me as a patient. Carol thought I might have used an assumed name, so she had long, detailed conversations with all sorts of facilities. But for obvious reasons, the cancer story never held up. There were no medical records anywhere to confirm it.

After speaking to my sister, Keawe called Erin, and they went into my Maui apartment to do a thorough search. They found my ice pipes and the sex tape that my dealer had made. They also found the dealer's name and address. They had no way of knowing he was a drug dealer, but when they background-checked him, they did find the restraining order filed by his ex-wife, so they were concerned. MPD began an official missing persons investigation and put Detective Keopu in charge of it.

Around this time, my mom received a phone call from my landlady looking for the rent, which I hadn't paid in a couple of months. My mom flew to Maui, and when she got to my apartment, she was shocked to see the blue investigative gloves everywhere. Meeting with Keawe and Erin, she learned for the first time that Keawe was my boyfriend, something he was still concealing from Detective Keopu and the rest of MPD. Everyone now knew about the drugs. Together with Detective Keopu, my mom contacted the Everett Police Department and asked them to send an officer to the dealer's house for a welfare check.

The dealer had spent a lot of time telling me that my mother hated me, that Keawe hated me, so when that officer showed up at the door—a female from EPD—I learned for the first time that my family was looking for me.

"I'm here to see Miss Allison Moore," the officer said. "Are you Allison Moore?"

"Yes, she is," the dealer said. I was hovering in the background, not sure if he wanted me there or not.

Upstairs, the cats howled.

"Is that a—baby?" asked the officer.

"Just some cats," the dealer said, and the officer nodded.

"I need to ask Miss Moore a few questions," she said.

"Sure," the dealer said. I moved toward him, and the three of us stood outside the front door.

"Your mother is concerned about you, Miss Moore," the officer said. "Are you okay? Do you want to leave?"

"Of course not," I said. I was shocked that my mom was concerned. I thought she hated me. I didn't want to leave—I thought I had it pretty good here. The dealer was the only one who loved me, the only one taking care of me. If I left, where would I go?

The dealer laughed. "That's crazy," he said.

"I'd like to hear it from Miss Moore, please," the officer said.

"My mom," I said. "She can be a little . . . a little dramatic. If I haven't called her in a few days she thinks I've been kidnapped." I laughed nervously.

"So you are not being held against your will?" the officer said.

I looked at the dealer out of the corner of my eye.

"Of course not," I said.

"So tell me, why haven't you called your mother?" the officer asked, adopting a chattier, let's-be-friends tone.

"She's an adult, ma'am," the dealer said. "Her mother doesn't need to keep tabs on her."

The officer shook her head. "I'm just doing my job." She had no way of knowing he was a drug dealer, of course, and even if she had a search warrant, she would never have found anything in that house. He kept everything so well hidden that even I couldn't find his drugs. Believe me, I had tried.

The officer turned to me. "So there's no problem?" she asked. "You're fine?"

"I'm fine," I said, and she left. She had only been there a few minutes and had never even gone inside the house. She didn't separate the two of us like I was trained to do in a domestic case, and I was too terrified to say anything against the dealer in his presence.

The officer would report back to MPD and my mom that I appeared to be "adult and well." She believed me to be at the dealer's house voluntarily, and in a way I was.

In a way I was.

"Your mother's a fucking mental case," the dealer said, once the officer was gone.

"You told me she didn't want to see me," I said. "If she's looking for me, obviously she does."

"I doubt that."

"I better call her."

"She doesn't want to talk to you," he said. "She hates you."

I went upstairs, walking quickly by the door to the cat room. Sometimes the dealer would threaten to put me in the room with the cats in the dark. It felt silly to be so scared of baby cats, but I was. I knew they would attack me, claw me, and I wouldn't be able to catch them. It was all I could think about when I passed that room.

I found my bag in the bedroom and started looking through it. I couldn't find my phone.

"Where's my phone?" I called downstairs to the dealer.

"How should I know?"

"I can't find it. What did you do with it?"

"I didn't do anything with it. You probably lost it."

"Bullshit. I didn't lose it."

"You can't keep track of anything," he said.

I searched through my bag over and over again, and in doing so realized that my badge and ID were also missing. "Where did you—" I started to yell to him, but he cut me off.

"Come down and get me a drink, will you?" he yelled up the stairs.

I went downstairs and fixed him a drink just as he liked it—five ice cubes, vodka poured to exactly an inch below the top of the glass—and brought it to him in the shop.

"What is this?" he asked.

"Your vodka."

"I didn't want this," he said, throwing the drink on the floor.

"You just asked for it," I said.

"You're crazy," he said. "You can't get anything right. Clean up this mess."

I bent down to scoop up the ice cubes, and his boot came crashing down on my head. My ears rang from the pain, but as he lifted the boot up again, I was able to get to my feet and run toward the stairs. I had a head start because he was coming from a seated position. I made it to the bathroom, where I closed the door and locked it, hoping he would calm down and then I could come out.

Things became very quiet. He wasn't yelling, he wasn't calling my name, but suddenly I heard the key turn in the lock and he was there in the bathroom, pushing me down, forcing my head into the toilet bowl and holding it there.

I had a mouth full of water and was sputtering, trying to get my head up.

I'm dead, I thought.

Good.

Abruptly, he let go of my head, and I lifted it up, gasping, while he turned and walked away.

"I know you hid my phone somewhere," I yelled, as soon as I could talk again.

With my ID, my badge, and my phone all gone, I had nothing to connect me to the world outside that house. Nothing to prove I even existed.

If there was nothing to prove I was alive, I might as well be dead.

21

It was at this point that I decided to use his gun to shoot myself.

But him first.

When I couldn't find the bullets for the revolver, when he found me in the shop with it, he grabbed the gun and said, "What the fuck were you going to do with that?"

I dissolved. I could barely speak. "I just want to die," I said quietly. "Why won't you let me die? Please let me die."

He said nothing. He turned and walked away.

Over the next few hours, I waited for a beatdown. I tried to be very nice—*Can I get you a drink, can I iron your clothes?*—thinking he might go gentle with me. I also tried to think of other ways to kill myself.

I thought about using a kitchen knife, but by this time he had taken away all the sharp knives in the house. I looked for tools in the shop. I thought about getting up on the roof and diving head-first into the concrete. Would the fall be enough to kill me?

The beating never came.

He found another way to punish me.

The following day, his friend Joe was over, and the three of us smoked a lot of dope together. I never wanted Joe to leave because I knew afterward I would pay for looking at Joe or talking to him about something I shouldn't have. But this time, Joe left and nothing happened.

Then another guy appeared, a guy I'd never seen at the house before.

"I'm going out," the dealer said. That's what he always said when he went to do a deal or work a job and didn't take me. I didn't pay any attention. I was wandering around the house high, not giving any thought to this guy. The dealer almost always left me with some-one when he went out. Usually Tiffany or Joe, but sometimes just a random babysitter who would make sure I didn't leave. This guy was fat and middle-aged, in polyester pants and a buttoned-down shirt that was too tight for him. He looked like he had come straight from work. He wore a stupid-looking tie and a wedding ring.

I walked into the kitchen, and the next thing I knew I was fight-ing this guy off!

"Get off me, you fucker!" I yelled. He attacked even more sav-agely.

I couldn't believe what was happening. He was shoving me, slapping me, ripping at my clothes. I gave him one big shove and sprinted up the stairs to the bedroom. I hid in the shower, holding the handle shut, but when he found me, he was stronger and able to pull me out of there.

He threw me on the bed while I fought as hard as I could to get him off me. He pinned me down. He was a big man, fat, greasy.

He had a very hairy chest and a horrible smell. I was aware he was raping me, but I was focusing on his sweat dripping on my face. It was disgusting, and I struggled to turn my head to the side to get away from his sweat. He grabbed me by the hair on top of my head and made me look at him.

"I like your flesh," he said. Not skin. Flesh.

As soon as he finished and got off me, I ran for the bathroom and hid in the shower. The guy stayed in the house afterward, and when the dealer came home he found me still in the shower, crying.

"That asshole raped me," I said. I was sure the dealer was going to kill the guy, but he just looked at me and said, "I thought you liked rough sex with Keawe."

The guy walked up behind him then, and they just kind of laughed at me.

Then two hours later, another man. This time the dealer took the handle off the glass shower door so I couldn't hide in there anymore.

The men kept coming, and finally I realized I should stop fighting. That's what they were paying for, that's what they wanted. It wasn't much fun for them when I just lay there.

I have no idea how many men there were. I detached myself from what was happening and waited for my punishment to be over.

The second-to-last guy—he couldn't go through with it. He looked in my eyes, and I could tell he lost his nerve.

"Jesus," he said. "What the fuck am I doing?" He let me go and sat on the side of the bed. He lit a cigarette and offered me one.

"No, thanks," I said, thinking, *This man is so nice, I just want him to take me home.*

"I'm sorry," he said. "I'm just not into this."

"Me neither," I said. "Listen, I need to get out of here. Can you take me with you?"

"Can't do that," he said.

"Please," I said. "I'll do anything. You can do anything you want."

He shook his head.

"Please take me with you."

"I've got a family," he said, and walked out of the room. He couldn't rape me, but he wouldn't rescue me either.

The next guy, the last guy, he was the roughest. After slapping me around a bit and raping me, he started to choke me. I felt like I was about to pass out, and I tried to remember what they taught us at recruit school to try to make your neck as tight as you can. I struggled to get my fingers under his hands, and then I blacked out. When I woke up—I'm sure I was only out for a second—my dealer was beating the guy.

My twisted thought was, *Wow, he loves me. He really loves me.*

The men stopped coming after that.

I have no idea where these men came from. Probably he found them on the Internet. I know they paid him for their privileges, but they weren't there for the dealer's gratification. It's not like he had an appetite for watching men do that. He just did it to punish me. I knew the cameras were recording all the rapes, but I doubted he would watch them. The porn he enjoyed was not sadistic, though he might find ways of selling this footage to men who did enjoy rapes.

Later, when I was sober, I began to fantasize about killing my dealer. I also thought about these men. The dealer was crazy. Barely human. A walking drug. I knew the dealer was insane, but these men—these supposedly normal men, who came into the house, did what they did to me, and left, made me more angry and infinitely more scared. These men—they went home to their wives.

22

It was around this time that MPD showed up: two internal affairs detectives, Keopu and Sommers. I had never met either of them until the day they appeared at the dealer's house.

I had been in the house only a month, but it had felt much, much longer.

I hid upstairs when I heard the doorbell. I was now terrified when someone new came into the house, terrified of what they were there to do. But as I listened to the conversation and heard my mom's name, Keawe's name, and Erin's, I moved from the bedroom and sat at the top of the stairs next to the cat room.

One of the detectives spotted me.

"Allison Moore?" he asked.

"Hi," I said.

"Can we talk to you for a moment?"

"Why don't you guys come in," the dealer said. He was arrogant enough to invite them into his drug house and not worry about being caught. Arrogant but accurate: there was nothing they would see or find that would concern them. It was a normal, suburban house and he was a normal, suburban man.

I slowly walked down the stairs and followed them into the kitchen, where we all sat around the kitchen table.

"Do you want a beer?" the dealer asked the detectives.

"No, thanks," one of them replied.

They held out their hands and introduced themselves to me. "I'm Detective Keopu," the older one, the Hawaiian one, said. "And this is Detective Sommers." They weren't wearing uniforms, but both produced their badges to show me.

"I know why you're here," the dealer said. "She's an addict. Has been for a long time. Her problems started long before I met her. Back when you guys were supposed to be taking care of her. I'm just trying to get her clean."

"Is that true?" Detective Keopu asked. The dealer got up from the table and stood in the doorway glaring at me.

"Yes," I said, admitting to MPD for the first time what I should have told them almost two years ago.

"Is it ice?" Keopu asked.

"Yes."

"You know the department can get you help."

"I'm helping her," the dealer said. His act made me so angry. And his confidence—he was taking control of them just as he had taken control of me.

"Your mother would really like you to come home," Keopu said. "Do you think you want to do that?"

"No," I said. "I'm good."

They talked to us for a long time, maybe a half hour. At one point they did try to separate us, but the dealer was too smart for that. He stood in the doorway, threatening me with his eyes. And I let him—this monster who just days before had let men come into his house and rape me. I could see he wasn't even worried. He knew I wouldn't say anything.

The detectives really had no power here, and he knew it. All they could do was talk.

I just wanted them to go so I could ask the dealer for some dope.

Suddenly, Sommers looked right at me and said, "Do you want to leave with us? If you want to come home with us, you can come home right now."

I looked at the dealer. "No," I said, after a minute. "I'm happy here."

Detective Keopu, this man who didn't even know me but cared about me because I was his sister in blue, looked very sad. He nodded his head slowly and said, "Would you at least call your mother?"

"I can't," I said. "My phone—"

"You can give her mother my phone number," the dealer said. "We'd be happy to talk to her."

Pompous asshole, I thought. He was convinced he was smarter than everybody else in the room.

After they left, I was badly punished, whipped on my bare back with a hose.

Eight miles away, at my sister's house in Snohomish, Keopu and Sommers were having a barbecue with my family. They were trying to strategize how to get me to leave that house. Everyone knew that I was an addict, but because I was an adult, they couldn't force me to leave.

"We could all be charged with kidnapping if we try to forcibly remove her," Keopu told my mom.

"Then what can we do?" my mom asked. "We have to get her out of there."

"You're going to have to convince her to come home."

Keopu brokered a conversation between my mom and the dealer, and she called him a couple of days later. He talked to her for a long time and put me on the phone briefly.

"I'm coming," she said. "I'm coming to see you and bring you home."

"No," I said. "I can't come home, Mom. I'm sorry."

"I'm coming," she promised. "I'll be there tomorrow."

It wasn't tomorrow. It was days later than that—I found out later that the dealer kept rescheduling and putting her off. Controlling the situation.

Meanwhile, he kept doling out punishments to me. One time he came out of the cat room with a trash bag and threw it at me. I caught it instinctively. Through the plastic I could feel that I was holding two dead kittens.

"Here's rotten pussy," he said. "Just like yours."

I don't know what he did to them. I suppose he broke their necks. Maybe they starved to death.

He also began to punish me by withholding dope. This was his first mistake, maybe his only mistake. I could recover from any beating, but I couldn't live without dope.

I started searching for dope everywhere. Whenever he went into the shop, whenever he was busy with negotiations downstairs, I would examine every light socket, every drawer, every cabinet within my reach. I knew what a risk I was taking by doing this. The cameras were recording me all the time, and at any moment he could have watched the footage and seen what I was doing.

I didn't care. I needed dope.

• • •

Six days after I spoke to my mom, the dealer finally let her come see me. "Oh Alli," she said. "You're so thin, honey. You really look like you need help."

He hadn't told me she was coming, and he'd gotten me so high right before she arrived that I could barely speak.

Seeing my mom was like the shock of jumping into a cold lake. It wasn't pleasant. I didn't want to see her. I was too far gone for that. There was no returning to a life where I'd been somebody's daughter, somebody's little sister. My life—what was left of it—was with the dealer now. That was all I had.

She brought me some shoes and warm clothes because Detective Keopu had told her I looked like I was freezing. The clothes smelled like the detergent my mom used. They smelled like home.

The dealer laid out the bullshit again, telling my mother how much he loved me, how he knew I was an addict, but he was determined to help me get sober. He let her take us out to lunch, and he kept his hand on my kneecap the entire time, squeezing it tighter and tighter as he suspected I would blurt out anything that contradicted his lies.

"Please come with me, Alli," my mom said when she dropped us back off at the house. "Please come home. We'll get you help. It's going to be all right."

I wanted to leave so badly. I just wanted my mom to pick me up and carry me out of that house. But I didn't say anything. I didn't say a word.

The dealer said to my mother, "I love your daughter. I love Alli, and whatever troubles she has started a few years before she met me. I'm just trying to take care of her."

My mom gave him a tight-lipped smile. "I think I can take better care of her at home," she said.

"That would be fine, but it seems like she wants to stay right here with me. That right, Alli?"

I nodded and said in my small, Minnie Mouse voice, "YES."

I knew it sounded strange and wasn't right, but I just couldn't leave. I was too afraid. In one way all I wanted to do was get out of that house, but in another way I knew it was too late for me. This was who I was now, an addict, a prisoner, a whore. I had destroyed too much of my old life to go back to my family who loved me.

I chose the drug over my mother. Now my life *was* the drug, and I needed to stay where I could get it.

"If you really want to take care of her," the dealer said, "I could use a little help. Alli can't work, so I'm supporting her. Her groceries, her clothes . . ."

Money. He was asking my mom for money.

My mom had been advised by MPD to do whatever it took to keep the lines of communication open—even if it meant leaving the house without me. Had she known about the abuse and the rapes, she would have fought the dealer then and there. But she didn't know, and she wrote him a check for a hundred dollars and left.

I had made my choice, and as I looked out the window watching her drive away, I thought, *That's it. I'm never going to see my mom again.*

I expected to die in that house, but I figured I could get in a few good highs first. What I didn't know was that the survival instinct that had made me a good cop was still buried somewhere inside me, and despite everything, it would find a way to get out.

23

I remember very clearly the day I felt I could get out of that house.

Desperate for dope, I was crawling around on the Berber carpet upstairs, looking everywhere. I saw something white sticking out of an air vent, and as an addict, my thought was, *That's where he's hiding the dope.* I pried open the vent and found my ID.

My wallet and driver's license, my badge, my cell phone—they were all there. I knew I hadn't lost them like he said I had. He had kept them hidden from me. I held these things in my hands, reading my birth date on my license, looking at my picture. I was the person in the picture, the owner of the badge. These things were symbols of my freedom, my epiphany: I wasn't as bad as I thought. I hadn't lost them. He had hidden them. Seeing these things now—on my hands and knees, desperate for dope—made me feel as if I was discovering myself all over again.

I was real. I had been this person—somebody's daughter, somebody's sister, somebody's lover, somebody's friend. And just like that I knew I could build up the strength to be that person again.

I turned my cell phone on and like some kind of miracle, there was a sliver of battery and a signal. I quickly sent my mom a text telling her to pick me up on Friday at three forty-five, and then switched the phone off and put it back. The dealer had to do a big deal on Friday; I knew he wasn't going to be in the house for a couple of hours and would probably leave me with Tiffany, who I knew I could overpower if I had to. He had gotten lazy lately and taken to leaving me alone sometimes. Since he had started depriving me of dope, any time he left he gave me a good bit to keep me company. He knew I wouldn't get restless if I had enough good dope.

I hid the phone and all the other things back in the vent so he wouldn't suspect anything. I planned to check the phone later in the week to see if my mom had replied, but I never had a chance. When Friday came, I had no idea if she was coming, but I knew I was going.

The dealer left me alone with a bowl of meth and a packet of cocaine. I told him I was going to water the front lawn so he wouldn't get upset if he got a text saying the front door had opened.

I waited. If my mom didn't come, my plan was to head to the airport and find a john wealthy enough to put me up for a couple of nights in a hotel while I figured out what to do from there. Or if I had to, I would walk the eight miles to my sister's house and beg her to let me stay.

I waited until the last second to fill a small duffel bag with my belongings. I didn't have much to pack. I stuffed my pockets with the meth and coke the dealer had left me, put my things by the front door, and waited for three forty-five.

Three forty-five came and my mom wasn't there.

I flipped out. I knew the cameras in the house had seen me

packing, so I couldn't unpack. That was it. I didn't have a choice: I had to go.

I was super high and went to the refrigerator to get a beer to calm me down enough so I wouldn't start sprinting down the street. I chugged a whole beer, picked up my bag, and walked out the door.

As soon as I hit the driveway, I lost my nerve. I had been out of the house so rarely that it all felt terrifying. I would turn back, deal with the punishment. Who was I to think I could leave?

And then, like my hero, my mom came racing down the cul-de-sac in a red rental car. I couldn't believe she was there.

She got out of the car and ran to me, just wanting to hug me and hold me.

I was so scared. I looked up the street to see if his truck was turning in. "Mom," I said, "we have to go."

I threw my bag in the car and then we were driving. All I could think was, *He's chasing us.*

"I'm so high I can't think right now," I blurted out.

"It's okay, honey. I know, I understand. We're going to get you some help."

"The things that I've done, Mom, the person that I've been—"

"Shhhh, sweetheart. You're safe now."

My mom's phone rang and it was Keawe.

"I have her!" my mom said, and handed the phone to me.

"You did the right thing, Alli," Keawe said. "You're going to be okay."

He kept talking to me, but I couldn't pay attention to what he was saying. I was grateful to be hearing his voice, but I was too busy checking the back window to see if the dealer was behind us.

We drove straight to the airport, but there weren't any flights left to Albuquerque that evening. We would have to wait until morning.

I started to tremble. I wasn't going to be able to get out of Washington alive. He was already hunting me, and the airport was the first place he would go. It was over.

"Honey, you're shaking so bad," my mom said. "We'll get you help. You're safe now."

I nodded. I couldn't bear to tell her the truth: we were both dead. He was going to kill me, and he was going to kill her too.

My mom decided we would stay at a hotel near the airport. I wanted to tell her that the dealer was coming after us, but I didn't want to scare her. In my heart I knew he was coming. My eyes darted everywhere, looking for him.

When we got to the hotel, my mom, still in the midst of her alcoholism, wanted to go downstairs and have dinner. I was high out of my mind. And terrified. I could hardly speak to her yet I was trying to act normal. I wanted to please her, so I said, "Sure, let's go to dinner."

She had a lot of wine at dinner. She was so excited that we were reunited and kept chatting away. "We'll get through this," she kept saying. "We'll put this all behind you. You're coming home." At this point, she was talking only about the drugs, which as far as I was concerned wasn't my problem. She knew nothing about the monster she thought was a man.

I couldn't eat or drink because I knew what was coming. Afterward, we went back to the room, my mom passed out, and I lay down, waiting for him. I ran through all the scenarios in my mind:

He won't make it through that door before security comes.

If he gets to the door, I can call 911 before he breaks down the door.

If he gets in the room, I can use the lamp to kill him.

All night long.

Morning came, and he still hadn't found us. We went to the airport and checked in. We had two hours until the plane left, so to keep my mom safe, I decided I would go find the dealer before he found us.

"I have to go to the bathroom," I said. Instead, I started jogging all over the airport, looking for the dealer.

If you're going to kill me, just do it now, but don't kill my mom.

I couldn't find him. I knew he was there, somewhere, watching me, ready to kill me, but I couldn't find him.

I returned to my mom after twenty minutes, just as the plane was about to board.

"Alli!" she shrieked at me.

"What?" I asked. I couldn't figure out why she was so angry at me. Then I saw that she was pale and in tears. She thought that I had run, that I wasn't going to go with her, that she had lost me again.

"Alli," she said, "don't ever leave me like that again. Stay with me, honey. Stay with me." She held my hand, and we walked onto the plane together.

Within the half hour, the dealer still hadn't come.

The plane took off.

We were going to be all right.

24

Two days rescued, I was at home in bed hugging Bella, my mom's dog, when my mom came in and said, "You're going to rehab."

"Like hell I am," I said. No way was I going to rehab. The house was the problem, the dealer was the problem, not the drug. I loved meth and had no plan to stop using.

Lurching from bed, I backed into a corner, my eyes darting from door to windows to my mom. I was about to run and she knew it.

"Talk to Keawe," she said, handing me her cell phone. "Talk to him."

Crying, I called Keawe. It was only 6 a.m. in Maui, but he answered right away. My mom had obviously prepped him for my call.

"You can do this," he told me. "You need to do this. I know you're strong enough."

"I'm not," I said. "I'm not stopping."

"You have to," he said. "You have to get sober. If you can't do it for yourself, do it for me. Please."

I was squatting on the floor at this point, shaking and edgy from the meth I had just snorted.

"Get sober and we'll start over," Keawe said. "In California."

Our dream. We had been talking about California for a long time.

There was a silence and then he said, "I told Colleen."

"I don't believe you." I started to rock back and forth. Aware that my mom was watching my every move, I tried to stay still. I tried to keep myself from turning into a ball and rolling on the floor, rolling away. I knew I looked crazy. What must she think of me?

Keawe kept talking. "I told her about us, Alli. I told her everything."

"Everything what?"

"That I don't love her anymore. That I love you. That I'm moving out."

I couldn't even hold the phone anymore. I jammed it between my ear and shoulder and tucked my hands under my armpits. Rolling, rolling away.

"Do you hear what I'm saying, girl?" he asked, and suddenly I could picture his face as he said this, the tender, twitching corners of his smile, his warm brown eyes, his lovely, smooth skin. I hadn't seen him in . . . weeks? Months? I had no idea how long. Time had lost all meaning for me.

I smiled and nodded at him.

"Alli?"

I remembered that he couldn't see me. I had to say something. "Yes."

"I need you to do this," Keawe said. "I need you to get strong and healthy. I need *you*." I heard his voice break, and for a moment I actually did feel like the strong one.

Keawe's were probably the only words that would have gotten me to go to rehab that morning. I was pissed that this was being chosen for me, that I didn't have a say in what was happening. I wasn't about to admit I had any problem. I had left the dealer's house with my pockets stuffed with dope, for God's sake. I knew everything would be all right if I could only have one more hit. One more slam.

But for Keawe, I would go to rehab. For Keawe, I would try.

"You need to get dressed, sweetie," my mom said, handing me a T-shirt and a pair of jeans.

"These aren't mine!" I yelled, throwing them back at her. I hadn't brought anything with me from Seattle but a few dirty tank tops, flip-flops, and one pair of jeans.

"They'll be a little big, but they're the best we've got. I think your sister left them the last time she visited."

My mom shepherded me into the bathroom and pressed the clothes into my hands. "Splash some water on your face, sweetie," she said. "And give your hair a good brush."

I was acting like a teenager and my mom was acting mom-like. Except that when I was an actual teenager, she had been nothing like this. I couldn't remember her ever telling me what to wear or when to get ready. She had always been off in her own world, equal parts artsiness, wine coolers, and anger.

"Where are we even going?" I asked her.

"I've found a place that has agreed to take you," she said. "But we have to go today or they'll give the bed to someone else."

Turns out she had spent the morning calling rehab places all over Albuquerque, but every single one was full. The only facility that could take me was a fancy spa rehab called Vista in Taos, three and a half hours away.

I dove back into bed, covering myself with pillows. My mom sat next to me and patted my leg, not saying a word.

After a while I said, "Okay, I'll go. But if I'm going to make it to Taos, I'll need something to calm me down. I'll only go if you get me some Valium." I figured I could slip outside and smoke the last little bit of meth I had while she was at the pharmacy.

"Get dressed first," my mom said. I grabbed the clothes and went into the bathroom. I took off my pajama top and stood naked from the waist up. My eyes inched slowly toward the mirror. I had fresh bruises under my rib cage and long thin welts at the tops of my thighs. He had been so careful where he pounded me.

As I bent over to shimmy off my pajama bottoms, I felt his hot, sour breath on my neck. I smelled his skin, his hair. Fists clenched, I whipped around to face him.

"No!" I shouted at him.

"What is it, honey?" Seeing the doorknob turn, I lunged at the door. "Don't come in," I yelled savagely. "Don't come in."

I pushed against the door with all the strength I had left, then pushed the lock shut. I couldn't let my mom see the bruises. If she didn't know about them, they weren't there.

"I'm okay," I told her. Needing a hit, I crouched on the floor to look for the meth I had hidden under the bathroom sink. Or thought I had. Maybe I had smoked it all, because there was nothing to find but a baggie of coke wedged behind the toilet. I shoved it in the pocket of the jeans.

Afraid I was going to cut and run, my mom sent Mimi, my eighty-two-year-old grandmother, to the pharmacy and put me in the car. My mom paced up and down the driveway, talking on the phone with the director of Vista Taos, clicking the door locks every time I tried to get out.

Soon my little Mimi came speeding down the driveway and got out of her car with a brown paper bag. She and my mom started passing the bag back and forth, looking into it and talking. It seemed like they were arguing, but finally my mom hugged Mimi, took the bag, and got in the car with me.

"Here you are, my dear," she said, handing two tablets to me and putting the car into reverse. She was already on the main road before I opened my eyes and saw that she had given me vitamins. Vitamins! As a cop, I could ID drugs right away. I had all the imprint numbers memorized.

"You amateurs," I said. I was so angry I started laughing. Mimi hadn't been able to get the Valium prescription, so they thought I could be tricked into going to rehab with goddamned *valerian root*?

Didn't matter. The cocaine in my pocket would get me through the next couple of days, and I didn't intend to stay any longer than that.

I fought to remain in my seat on the way to Taos. I squirmed, called Keawe at work three or four times just to hear his voice, listened to my mom chatter about how proud she was of what I was doing, how great things would be when I was "better." Understand, she still had no idea of the extent of what had happened to me in Seattle, and as far as I was concerned, she would never know. I planned never to tell a soul about the horrors of that house.

Halfway to Taos we stopped at a Circle K so my mom could get some caffeine. I could tell she was itching for a drink. Willpower wasn't her strong point, but she was driving and would settle for a coffee.

I got out of the car and looked around. She had deliberately chosen to stop somewhere off the highway, nowhere near a town. If I tried to run, there was nothing but desert all around. I would have to sprint all the way back up to the highway and see if I could hitch a ride before she got to me.

"I have to pee," I said.

"Okay," she said. She followed me to the bathroom, and I half expected her to come inside with me, just like when I was a little girl. She opened her mouth to say something, then waved me in by myself.

After I peed, I figured I had enough time to do a line of coke. I pulled the packet out of my pocket and looked around the filthy bathroom for a flat surface. Still high from all the meth I had snorted that morning, I caught sight of myself in the mirror. It was one of those gas station mirrors that isn't even really a mirror, just some unbreakable acrylic silver thing in which you can barely see the shape of your own face. Plus it was spattered with dried soap and some scummy orange stuff. Looking at myself in that mirror—trying to see myself at all—I can't say I had a moment of clarity, but I did make a decision.

"Alli," my mom called, pounding angrily on the door. "Come out of there right now. We've got to get going."

"Just a minute," I said, and then I did something I still find hard to believe.

I threw that packet of cocaine away.

I buried it deep in the trash can, under a pile of brown paper towels.

That's it, I thought. *I'm done*. I didn't finish the coke. I didn't try to sneak it into rehab. I just threw it away. I hadn't chosen rehab, but I did choose sobriety for myself on that day.

I would do it. I would throw myself into it full-force. I suppose for someone like me, even sobriety can become a kind of addiction.

• • •

Very few addicts experience the kind of rehab I was given. Brand-new adobe-style buildings, gorgeous landscaping, king-size beds, fluffy towels. As we pulled up to Vista in the car, I thought my mom had been joking with me and wasn't really taking me to rehab after all. It looked like a resort for rich people, not a place for drug addicts. Turns out it was costing my mom twenty thousand dollars for thirty days. I was still so focused on myself that I couldn't appreciate that my family had gotten that much money together in a single morning for my treatment.

Bill, the head of Vista, came out to greet me, acting as if he had been waiting for me the entire day.

"We're so glad you're choosing sobriety, Alli," he said, and took us into his office. He rattled off a bunch of other rehab bullshit about group sessions, primary treatment, complementary therapies, and other stuff I didn't listen to. I stared at the painting above his desk. A peaceful river painted in thick brushstrokes. A hint of blue sky in the distance. Sun.

Bill asked me for the names and addresses of people I wanted to invite to Family Week, the last week of treatment. My mom gave him her address and my sister Carol's. It didn't occur to us to give him my father's. I gave Bill Keawe's address, sure that he would want to come.

Suddenly Bill said, "Say good-bye to your mother, Alli."

I turned to my mom with panicked eyes. "What? Already?"

She hugged me and started to cry. "This is how they do things, sweetie," she said.

"I need you, Mom," I said. "I just got back to you."

"It's important to find your own journey through sobriety," Bill said. "After three days you can call your family."

"Don't leave me," I said, clinging to my mom, burrowing my thin, bony frame into the soft roundness of her body. I felt panic rise through my chest, my throat. I was twenty-eight years old but felt about seven. Suddenly I was convinced that my mother, who I had done nothing but lie to and avoid for two solid years, was the only one who could keep me safe.

Bill gently pulled me away and led me down a long, tiled hallway to the huge room with four beds where I would be staying all by myself. I felt like the smallest little person in the world.

He left me alone in my room. It was a beautiful room—fourteen-foot ceilings, a fireplace—but I didn't care. I was worried about the door out to my own little porch. I checked the door four or five times to make sure the dead bolt was locked. I was sure my dealer would track me to Taos and kill anyone at the rehab in order to get to me.

I was so tired. I felt like I hadn't really slept in years. Two years, at least. Going to bed at a normal time felt strange, but an orderly came in and started me on some drugs—trazadone to help me sleep; clonidine for anxiety and panic attacks (I wasn't given preferential treatment after I was diagnosed with PTSD); and the antidepressant Paxil, thought to help with meth cravings.

I woke up around midnight to go to the bathroom. As I walked across the room my heart started to beat so fast I thought I was having a heart attack. Dropping to my knees and then my stomach, I lay on the cold bathroom floor and prayed for my heart to slow down, begging God for it not to stop altogether. I knew if I could get a hit I would be all right. I decided my body couldn't survive without dope, and I was probably going to die.

Tears washed down the bridge of my nose and onto the tile floor. I wanted to call out to my mom to take care of me. Or Keawe. But

I couldn't even make a sound. All I could hear was my heartbeat. I had no idea what was happening to me.

Slowly, my heartbeat returned to normal. My body became responsive, and I felt better. I knew I would live. I crawled back to bed, but first I checked the lock on the door to the porch again. I should have gone to the night orderly and told him what had happened, but I was determined to keep it to myself.

I later found out I was experiencing the side effects of trazadone. If you try to get up too quickly, the drug can cause a rapid heartbeat and light-headedness. I was lucky I hadn't passed out.

In the morning, I awoke to find a man bending over me.

"Get the fuck away from me, you fucker," I screamed. I lunged at him, getting my hands around his throat within seconds.

He was strong, able to shove his hands under my grasp.

"Whoa there, Miss Allison," he said. "I'm not trying to hurt you." His voice was surprisingly gentle.

Thrashing around in the bed, I freed my legs from the sheets and started kicking him. He backed away, and I could see him clearly for the first time. A white guy, middle-aged. My worst nightmare.

"I'm Arnie," he said, again in that gentle voice. "Your orderly. I just came to wake you up."

"Oh God," I said, embarrassed. "I'm sorry. I thought you were—"

"Next time I won't get so close," he said, and he was true to his word. It became a standing joke between us: every morning after that, he woke me by standing in the doorway and poking me with a stick.

For three solid days it seemed I did nothing but sleep, take my medication, and go to the bathroom. I don't think I ate anything.

When I woke up that third morning, I was in the pink cloud of sobriety. I looked out the window at the roses on my porch and was sure I had never seen that color pink before. I stared at the beautiful little stream running through the grounds and absolutely could not believe what I was seeing. It was as beautiful as the painting in Bill's office.

Everything felt wonderful. I was going to be sober for the rest of my life.

When my counselor Greg came by that morning to give me my schedule, I said, "I got the shit out of my system, I'm good to go." He started laughing and couldn't stop.

Greg was there to start me on the "Vista routine." He had a clipboard, a schedule, and brochures, and he went over the things I had to do in the morning: up at seven, make your bed, brush your teeth, shower, go to breakfast, go to group. Every day, no exceptions. Starting now.

"Fine," I said. "Now. Okay."

Greg nodded, but he and his clipboard didn't leave.

"We find that new guests are sometimes resistant to our schedule," he said. "They see it as a bit of a regime. We find it's best to accompany our guests through each step of the routine the first day or two." He glanced at the clipboard. "First up, make your bed."

He lowered himself into the plum-colored suede easy chair in the corner of my room and watched me make my bed. I started to feel a little queasy by the end. What the fuck was the difference between rehab and Seattle? A middle-aged man telling me what to do every minute, then watching me do it.

"Good, Alli," Greg said once I had finished. "We want our guests to go through the motions of daily life, to meet the expectations that will be there when they move back into the world. Now it's time to brush your teeth, then a shower."

"You're going to come in the shower with me?" I asked.

"Of course not," he said. "I'll wait here."

I got out a change of clothes and went into the bathroom. I hadn't taken a shower in at least a week. I laid out one of Vista's luxurious white towels and even turned on the water, but there was no way I could make myself go in the shower. Not after Seattle, not after the men. I was terrified, but I didn't want Greg to know what was going on. I let the shower run while I washed my hair in the sink.

"Feel refreshed?" Greg asked when I came out of the bathroom.

I nodded, and he "accompanied" me to the dining room for breakfast, where the Mexican wood table was set with cloth place mats and beautiful stone-colored pottery in all different bright shades. Orange, turquoise, purple, yellow. A vase was filled with purple and yellow desert wildflowers. Platters of fresh pineapple and papaya sat in the middle of the table.

I took one look at the faces around the table and said a little prayer to Keawe—*Get me out of here*. That's all I wanted. To be with Keawe, headed for California.

Greg sat next to me and tried to get me to contribute to the conversation, but I was silent while I tried to choke down some tea and a piece of dry toast. *This fucking shit is for the birds*, I thought. *I'm sober now, can I just leave?* Some woman was talking about how she didn't want to go outside because of all the spiders at Vista. Another woman was complaining about the chipped nail polish on her toenails. Apparently they felt they were slumming it. What did a vice cop meth addict have in common with a woman who was more concerned with going thirty days without a pedicure than getting sober?

I was the only meth addict at Vista, I learned a few minutes later in group. The others were mostly alcohol or heroin. Julianne, a gallery owner from Santa Fe who always drank too much at art openings. Christian, a heroin addict, cutest little skater kid in the whole world. Meg, a middle-aged mom who couldn't stop using painkillers after a skiing accident. Shira, a college student whose parents were concerned about her partying and bad grades. Sam, a middle-aged white guy with cold eyes and a strong appetite for heroin. Diana, an alcoholic from California, an actress I was pretty sure I had seen in something once.

As we went around the circle and talked, I started to fall asleep, which the counselors tolerated, knowing that I was detoxing. Suddenly the craving for meth hit my body like a semi.

"*I need dope!*" I wanted to scream, yell, run from the room.

I clutched the edges of my seat and started to rock back and forth to keep myself from running out the door. I didn't know where I was going to go or how I was going to get meth, I just knew that I had to run out of that room. Everything in my body was screaming for me to do something. It took all my strength to sit in that chair and endure that craving. It seemed like hours, but I think it was less than thirty minutes before the craving went away.

There would be more cravings, but this would be the worst. The others would come and go in a matter of minutes, and I would learn to deal with them.

When I was finally able to loosen my grip on the chair and look around the circle again, I found Sam staring at me. I looked down at my wet hair, my tank top, tried to cover myself. All middle-aged white guys were threats to me now.

At dinner that night, Sam sat next to me. "I got this for you," he said, and handed me a Suboxone. Suboxone is a big thing in rehab. It's kind of like methadone, used a lot with heroin addicts. We were all given different meds, all nonaddictive drugs, but some of them can get you high, and Suboxone is one of them. I didn't know what to do, so I accepted it, but with the Suboxone in my pocket, I felt I wasn't safe anymore. I was in a place where I could still get drugs if I wanted them.

I went back to my room, my heart pounding, and flushed the pill. I didn't hesitate even a moment.

It gave me a lot of self-confidence to flush that pill. I couldn't wait to tell Keawe what I had done. I had earned my first phone call that night, and I headed to the phone room for my allotted ten minutes.

"Hey, you," he said. His voice was so tender a sob rose in my throat.

"I miss you so much," I said.

"Me too. How are you doing?"

I barely wanted to talk. I just wanted to hear his voice saying my name over and over again for those precious ten minutes.

"Is the rehab working?" Keawe asked. "Do you feel like you're getting better?"

I told him about the pill, about Sam.

"Just stay away from him," Keawe advised. "Isn't there someone else you can hang out with?"

I pictured all the women from group. "No," I said. "They're all too . . ." And then I thought of Christian, eighteen, practically a little kid. Plus he'd been using heroin for three years, so he was probably fifteen at heart. He wasn't a threat to me.

"There's this skater kid," I said. "He's like a little brother."

"Stick with him," Keawe said.

I had been waiting so long to talk to Keawe, but things felt almost worse now that I had. All I could think about was getting back to him.

That night, after checking the locks in my room more than a dozen times, I lay in my bed and cried from missing him. Keawe was the one good thing I had been able to hang on to while I threw myself into hell. I felt sure that if only he were with me, he could make the dealer go away.

The next morning before breakfast, I tried again to take a shower. I turned the water on and took my nightgown off, then hugged myself to keep warm while I worked up the nerve to go in.

Suddenly, the dealer was there in the bathroom with me. *Get me a drink*, he said in my ear. I smelled his vodka breath on my neck. I whipped around, crashed into the wall trying to get away from him, and then collapsed onto the floor.

I missed breakfast and was late for group because I literally couldn't move from the bathroom for half an hour. How could I share any of this? Sitting in group listening to these women talk about how they had one too many glasses of wine while they played mah-jongg made me feel like such an outsider. It's not that I didn't want to fit in. I did, but I wasn't about to tell anyone what had happened in Seattle.

These secrets, they ate away at me. They were breaking me, they were killing me. I was so sick of secrets, and yet that's all I had. Once, I had had the opportunity to have a wonderful, normal life, and now I never would. It was over. I was done. I would carry on being detached and cold, pretending none of these things had happened. My meth use had always been about selfishness and avoidance, and so far sobriety hadn't changed that. Selfishness and avoidance.

At lunch, I looked for Christian, but he wasn't there yet. I found a seat between Julianne and Shira, and in less than a minute Sam came over and sat across from me. I closed my eyes, willing him to disappear.

Rage boiled in my throat. I hated Sam. I grabbed the knife from my place setting and flew at Sam, plunging it straight into the base of his neck. It went in fast and deep and I gave a little gasp, almost of pleasure. It was so easy. I pulled the knife out and went at him again. The blade slipped in a little higher this time, near his Adam's apple. Strings of blood spattered everywhere.

Opening my eyes, I looked directly into Sam's face. He was taking a bite out of the tortillas they were serving for lunch.

I mumbled, "Excuse me," and got up from the table.

It had felt so real. Completely real—my need to stab him convinced me that I actually had.

I stumbled back to my room, checked the door lock a few times, and lay down on my bed.

I was crazy. Flashbacks, now hallucinations. I was still seeing the dealer everywhere. *Get me a drink*, he would say, or *Go run the shower*. His breath, his smell, the terror of what would come next. How was I ever going to get over this?

In refusing to tell my counselors what was happening, in refusing to deal with any of it, I missed an opportunity to get better, and instead kept myself living in the dealer's house.

By my third week at Vista, my counselor Janice was fed up with my silence, my noncompliance. I would go to the breakfast table but I wouldn't eat. I would go to group but I wouldn't speak. I didn't want to talk about meth, think about meth or anything that had to do with drugs, yet twenty-four hours a day I had to talk, think, and learn about addiction.

When the orderlies came to offer me massages or aromatherapy, I always turned them down. I couldn't bear to have anyone touch me. At nine o'clock every night I would think, *My God, I have to go to bed soon and I can't do it*. And when it was three in the morning and I had lain awake all those hours, I just wanted the sun to rise so I didn't have to go to sleep and fight the dealer again. If I did fall asleep, my nightmares were so bad I peed the bed.

One morning in group, Janice made all the men leave the room and then turned to me with imploring eyes.

"Alli," she asked, "what are you hiding? What happened to you?"

Immediately I became nauseated and light-headed. I looked around the small circle of women. How could I tell them what had happened to me? They all had nice clothes, expensive homes, husbands or parents who cared about them. What in the world would they have in common with a meth-addicted cop who had become the prisoner of a drug dealer?

As always, I looked for a way out. And then I took a deep breath. "Things got very bad with this dealer I knew in Washington," I said. "He used to, he sometimes, you know, he raped me. And after a while he wouldn't let me leave."

I hoped this was enough. I didn't want to say any more. But the way they were looking at me, I was suddenly terrified that they would start asking questions: *Why couldn't you leave? Did he force you to take the drugs? Aren't you a cop—didn't you know how to overpower him?* These were all questions I couldn't yet answer for myself. There were so many things about Seattle that I hadn't even begun to explain, or understand.

In order to avoid their questions, I kept talking. "He kept me high on cocaine and meth all day, every day. I didn't know where I was. I barely knew *who* I was."

I told them as much as I was capable of at the time, which wasn't much. I didn't tell them about the beatings. I didn't tell them about the men. Afterward, the talking left me so shaken that Janice let me go to bed. She gave me a couple of clonidine to calm me down, and I slept for a day and a half. When I got up at six the next evening, I was surprised that I felt a tiny bit . . . *better?*

I felt excited, somehow, as if I had a secret I actually wanted to share. A completely new feeling for me. I still had one ten-minute phone call left that week, and I used it to call Keawe. I wanted to tell him that for practically the first time in my life, I had shared.

But when Keawe answered the phone his voice was ice cold.

"What's up?" I asked uncertainly.

"I can't talk to you, Alli," he said.

"I won't be able to call again for four days," I said. "Please—"

"No," he said. "I can't talk to you anymore. *Ever.*"

"Why? What are you talking about?"

"Colleen found out about us. I'm sorry, but I can't talk to you. Don't call anymore."

"But you told her," I said. "You said she knew. California . . ."

"I just said that to get you to go to rehab," he said. "And then I get this letter from that place you're at, inviting me to come to Family Week. Family Week! Jesus Christ, Alli. She opened it and went ballistic. What were you thinking, having them send that letter?"

"You told me she knew about us, you told me—"

"I'm sorry, but it was never going to happen. I have to stay with my family."

"What?" I whispered. I started trembling and tried to hold on to the phone.

"I could never leave them." *Not for* you *anyway*, I heard in his voice.

"Keawe, please—"

"I'm sorry," he said. "I wish you all the best, I really do, but—"

Before he could finish, my shaking hands dropped the phone.

Other people besides me can lie.

25

It seems miraculous to me now that I didn't start using again after Keawe broke up with me. That I didn't cut and run, find my way back to the dealer, and let him finish me off.

Keawe's words had shattered me, destroyed every ounce of self-esteem I had won back. I had gone to rehab for him, stayed there for him, and now he was gone from my life.

Family Week was excruciating without him. My mom expected him to be there, so I had to tell her what happened. Over the phone, she kept telling me it was going to be okay, but she was shocked. She saw him as my hero, my rescuer, and thought it was unbelievable that he would do this.

Carol's feeling were not so generous.

"The guy is just not there for you," she said. "He never shows up."

"Carol!" my mom scolded her. "Keawe was instrumental in finding Alli."

"Yeah, but how did he know she was with a drug dealer if he didn't know she was on drugs? It doesn't make any sense."

They bickered about Keawe as we waited for our first family session to begin. Carol was deeply suspicious of Keawe and his motives. I had no idea what to think about him anymore. Except that I still loved him desperately.

My mom and my sister looked so tired and pale. It was apparent what I had put them through, but I wasn't thinking about that at the time. I was thinking about myself.

I was so shocked that my sister had even come. I couldn't understand how she could forgive me, and in a way I didn't believe it.

My contact with Carol and my mom was surprisingly limited during Family Week. They had lots of educational sessions with other people's family members. We shared only a few sessions together. Carol and my mom hadn't had time to process what I had done to them, and now they were being forced to talk about it in a circle with strangers. Compared to the others, my family was wonderful. My friend Julianne's father was there, and he shouted, "My daughter doesn't have a disease! She's just weak morally."

I was barely four weeks sober during Family Week and still had a lot of the meth addict behaviors. I twitched and bounded in my chair. My eyes darted everywhere. My mom and sister saw me in a light they had never seen me in before.

Things between Carol and me were very strained. She was having a hard time forgiving me for the danger I had put her family and her daughters in—and she still didn't know the half of it. No one did.

My mom was her usual upbeat self, happily and naïvely assuming I was now "fixed" after a month in rehab. For her sake, I desperately wanted to believe I could be fixed, but even my own delusions couldn't take me that far.

After one of the family sessions, my counselor Greg pulled my mom aside and said, "I know you really want to help Alli."

"Of course I do."

"Well, if you really want to help her, you're going to have to stop drinking."

My mom looked stricken. "Has Alli been talking about—"

Greg shook his head. "She hasn't said a word. But I know you're a drinker. I can recognize it, and you have to stop."

Greg's words shocked my mom to the core. He was trained in addiction and spotted the signs—her broken capillaries, her swollen ankles, her barrel chest. My mom was mortified. Like me, she had thought that life with an addiction was manageable, that no one really knew about her alcoholism. She had quietly drunk herself into oblivion every night for ten years, but she was very secretive about her disease and very high-functioning. No one had called her on it. As far as I know, all her family and friends accepted my mom's drinking as harmless.

But Greg's words—his naming of her problem—made my mom quit drinking. That very day. I had stopped using on the sixth of September, and on the sixth of October she stopped drinking—a month to the day after I had thrown away the packet of cocaine in the gas station bathroom. From then on, we would celebrate our sobriety together on the sixth day of each month.

Vista desperately wanted to keep me another month, but my family couldn't afford the fees. Instead, at the end of Family Week I moved into Sober Living, an extended-care program housed in a rambling hacienda just off the main Taos square. It was called Casa Feliz—"Happy House"—and I was going to be living there with four girls all a little farther along in the sobriety process than I was.

In Sober Living I had a local sponsor, Barb, and had to go to Narcotics Anonymous meetings in the community all the time. I also had more freedom, more real-life perks, than at Vista. A house mom provided constant supervision, and there was lots of group and individual therapy, but they made it clear that I was there voluntarily. They couldn't keep me there. If I wanted to leave, well, there was the door. That freedom terrified me.

At Casa, I had Internet access and was allowed a cell phone, both of which made me feel more vulnerable. My mom bought me a phone the day she moved me into Casa.

"It's pay as you go," she told me. "Now, I don't want you running up a huge phone bill."

"Who would I call?" I asked. I was completely serious. I had no friends left. I had alienated every single person I had ever known on Maui. I had betrayed all of them for drugs.

They say sobriety is like waking up from a coma, and for me it was true; I had disappeared from my life for two years. Now that I was awake, I missed my friends badly, yet I could never have them back. I had betrayed them in the worst, most hurtful way. The pain consumed me, and when my mom left me alone to unpack at Casa, I just stared at that cell phone and the four numbers she had programmed into it—hers, Carol's, Mimi's, and my aunt's—and felt so grateful that my family had not abandoned me. They had every right to.

And then I called Keawe. Of course I had his phone number memorized, but mine was unfamiliar to him. He answered very tentatively.

"Hello?"

His voice—the way it hit me—suddenly, I could barely breathe.

"Hello?" he said again.

I gulped air and then forced out a couple of words. "It's me."

I expected him to hang up, but his voice was warm. "Alli. How are you doing?"

"I'm okay," I said. "I just wanted to see how you are."

"Getting by," he said. "Trying to keep my marriage together." He said this matter-of-factly, not accusingly. His voice didn't sound angry, and the fact that we were still talking suggested he wasn't.

"Are you getting better?" he asked me.

"Yes," I said. "Slowly. Four weeks sober."

"That's great."

"How's everyone at MPD? How's . . ."

"Fine," he said. "They're all fine. It's just that nobody understands . . . I don't understand. What the hell happened? Were you high the whole damned time we were together?"

"No!" I said. "Of course not."

"I just need to know," Keawe said, sounding a little lost. "I just need to know . . . some things, about what happened."

"I can't imagine what you're going through," I said. "I'll tell you everything. If you want me to."

"I've got to go," he said abruptly. "But you could email me, send me some of the details of how this all went down."

"Sure," I said. "I can do that."

"I think that's better than us talking," he said.

"Okay," I said. "I will."

We hung up just as my mom returned.

"How about some lunch?" she asked. "I've scouted out a great little place on the plaza."

"Okay," I said, and maybe I sounded too enthusiastic because she paused to look at me.

"This place agrees with you already, honey," she said. "You've got some color back into your cheeks." She put her arm around me, and we walked together to the restaurant.

It made me nervous, being around so many people. I surveyed the whole plaza. Looked behind me constantly. The dealer always liked to sneak up and push me without warning, and I had learned to always be aware of what was behind me.

We sat outside at a table with green umbrellas. It was a beautiful, bright October day and I felt I should be happy. I had been missing Keawe so desperately, and now I thought he might let me back into his life.

We had just finished eating when my cell phone rang. I was so pleased—I thought it might be Keawe again.

But it wasn't Keawe.

"Hi, Alli," a voice said.

Not the dealer.

The dealer's friend, Joe.

I slammed the phone down on the table.

"Who was it, honey?" my mom asked. "What's the matter?"

I shook my head.

"Was it him?" my mom asked.

I nodded.

"Damn him. Why can't he just leave you alone? Doesn't he understand you're done with all that?" She was referring only to the drugs. My mom still had no idea what the dealer had done to me, and I intended for her to never know.

My eyes scanned the plaza. Was he here? Was he watching me?

I didn't see him, but that didn't matter. He had found me. It would only be a matter of time before he came and got me.

How had he gotten this number? Had he tapped into my mom's email? My sister's email? Had he stolen her phone bill?

I didn't learn until later that he had been calling my mom, too, and messaging her on Facebook. She didn't want to alarm me, so she didn't tell me. He finally left her alone once she threatened to call the police.

Back at Casa that afternoon, we had a house meeting in the

kitchen. Our house mom, Lila, a tiny, gray-haired, motherly woman, was telling us about a roller derby team she thought we should all join. She put on a helmet and gave us her imitation of a roller derby queen. Laughing along with everybody, I turned away for a moment to pour myself a glass of milk, when out of nowhere the dealer appeared in front of me.

I screamed and threw the glass at him, but instead of hitting the dealer, who wasn't there, I hit the kitchen window. The glass broke, the milk spattered everywhere, and all my housemates knew there was something wrong with me. I was mortified.

"What's wrong, Alli?" Lila asked, while my roommate Josie and another girl started to clean up the mess.

"I am so sorry," I said. "I just—I have these flashbacks. I see things."

Lila patted my arm. "I'm sorry for this, honey. It must be very rough on you."

Everyone was so kind at Casa, and I tried to follow the rules, but I still wasn't talking in therapy. It was taking everything in me not to use. The other girls were all so much farther along in their recovery, and they weren't dealing with the same things I was. Now, with a roommate, I wasn't able to keep my severe nightmares and flashbacks a secret any longer. I would wake up in a panic and bolt across the room, scaring Josie, who did her best to calm me down. It wasn't really fair to her.

"I thought you were on meds for those," she would say drowsily as she tried to fall back to sleep after one of my episodes.

"I am," I said. "They just don't seem to be working."

Fed up, I stopped taking my meds. It was hard to tell if the hallucinations and nightmares got better or worse.

Keawe and I started emailing each other regularly. I knew it was a bad idea—he was putting his marriage back together, and

I needed to put Maui behind me. But once that door was opened again, I couldn't stay away

One night, about two weeks after I got to Casa, I was out in the courtyard with my computer, trying to email Keawe. I was wandering from wall to wall, trying to get a signal, when suddenly I heard a voice in my ear.

"You think Keawe still loves you, you cunt?" I looked up from the computer. There, in the bushes, was the dealer.

"No," I started screaming at him. "You leave me alone." I lunged toward him and collided with a stucco wall. The next thing I knew I was running into the house, my face cut up and bleeding.

"Hide me!" I screamed at Josie. The dealer was right behind me. I held on to Josie, and she started screaming and struggling to get away. I wanted comfort; she was terrified. All the lights went on, and everyone came to help Josie. "Get me away from him," I said, shaking them off as they tried to restrain me.

"He's going to get me," I yelled, careening around the room, dodging the dealer's blows. I had never had a hallucination that lasted this long. I was bleeding and wild-eyed.

Lila called the doctor. I was rambling, raving, incoherent. When the doctor showed up, he gave me a sedative right away.

"We need to 51-50 her," he told Lila.

Lila nodded grimly.

I knew good and well what that meant. The doctor had decided I couldn't make my own decisions and was sending me to the psych ward for an involuntary seventy-two-hour admission.

"Don't do that," I pleaded. "Just call my mom." But in the middle of all my ravings, no one was going to trust me.

The sedative knocked me out and I slept all night. First thing in the morning, Lila had to drive me to the Presbyterian Hospital psych ward, four hours away in Albuquerque. I begged her not to leave me there, and I could tell she felt bad about what had happened, but she had to get back to the other girls at Casa. She assumed I would be safe, staying in the psych ward until I normalized.

I was completely over my episode by the time I was admitted to the psych ward, and the sedative had worn off, so I was lucid, conversational, and funny. I managed to convince the doctors that everyone was overreacting, and they let me go after a few hours. They didn't bother to hold me for seventy-two hours like they should have; they didn't call my mom or even Lila. They let me walk out of the hospital. By myself. At eleven o'clock at night.

I wasn't sure what I was going to do. I could head to West Central, where I knew I could pick up. My meth cravings were so strong at that moment. But the Albuquerque drug scene was rough. Last time I had tried to pick up there, I had gotten robbed by a crack addict who stole my phone. I didn't want to deal with that shit.

By the grace of God, instead of going to use, I got in a taxi and went straight to my mom and Mimi's house.

I didn't have anything with me when I showed up at the door, just the small overnight bag Lila had packed for me before she took me to the hospital.

"Alli?" my mom said. "Honey, what happened?"

"I want to come home," I said, and started to cry.

She took me in her arms and brought me inside.

I spent the night at home and she drove me back to Sober Living the next day. I didn't want to go back. In my mind, I was done, and I only lasted a day or two before I called my mom to come pick me up again.

"No," she said. "You can't come home, Alli. You need to stay there." She was worried about my treatment, worried she couldn't handle me at home. She refused to come get me, and I didn't have enough money to get home by myself.

I left anyway. I went to my sponsor Barb's house, and she let me sleep on her couch. The next day, when my mom realized I was serious about leaving Casa, she picked me up and brought me home.

I never returned to Sober Living. Instead of using the opportunities presented to me there to talk about what had happened and to get better, I got to my mom's house and stopped functioning. I couldn't do anything but lie on my bed with Bella and watch cartoons. I never got out of my pajamas, I refused to see anyone, and I only left the house for therapy and doctor appointments.

The therapists discovered that my PTSD was among the worst they had ever encountered. They put me in intensive therapy and tried a new combination of meds, but I wasn't responding to therapy or to drugs very well. I couldn't sleep. I didn't know how to deal with the nightmares and the flashbacks, and so I did nothing.

All I could think about was the dealer coming after me. Or worse—I thought of him living in that house, carrying on exactly as before, only with someone else in my place.

I ached for the girl who might be in my place now. I knew from his recordings that I hadn't been the first, and there was no way to stop him from continuing to prey on other desperate addicts.

I knew there was nothing I could do for that girl. I couldn't just call the police department in Everett, Washington, and tell them to search the dealer's house for drugs or hidden cameras. As a former police officer, I knew what was needed to order a search warrant, and I didn't have it. By this point, the dealer would have encrypted all his videos anyway, so there would be nothing to find. I could have alleged abuse, but with no witnesses and no physical evidence, it would have been his word against mine.

Sometimes I thought if I could just get stronger and conquer the PTSD, I would be strong enough to go after him. I fantasized

about driving up there and killing him, but mostly I worried that he would find me and kill me first.

I found myself thinking back to the day I had planned to kill the dealer and myself. I wished there had been ammunition that day because sometimes, living with the aftermath, it was as if I was still there in that house.

And in a way, by not moving forward in my life, I was acting as if there had been bullets in that gun.

All I could say in my favor was that I was still alive and I wasn't using. These weren't small things, given my recent history, but they weren't enough to constitute a life. The truth was, I couldn't handle a life. My poor mom couldn't even work; she had to stay at home and watch me all the time. I felt like a broken person. No one could fix me.

I was no longer suicidal, but I felt into a deep, dark depression. I didn't even have enough energy to start using again. All I wanted to do was to stay in my own little cocoon in Mimi's back house and occasionally venture into the courtyard, completely shielded from the world, protected on all sides by stucco walls.

I would probably still be there, not moving even an inch forward in my life, if MPD hadn't come after me.

26

The day I was arrested, a man walked all the way down our driveway to give my mom a flyer for the hot dog stand on the corner.

"Now, why would he do that?" my mom asked me. "We pass that place every single day."

"Don't ask me," I said. My mom had been outside sweeping the walk while I was inside, lying on the couch, as usual. I didn't know anything about the outside world.

My mom frowned at me. "Honey, why are you back in your pajamas?"

"More comfortable," I said, shrugging.

That morning, at my mom's insistence, I had gone for an assessment at Pathways, a government-run program that helps addicts get back on their feet through funded therapy sessions and voucher programs for food and rent. I knew we needed the financial help, and so I had managed to put on clothes to leave the house for the appointment. Once I got home, I immediately returned to my normal attire. Pajama bottoms ripped at the thigh and duct-taped back together. A huge sweatshirt that went down to my knees. Tennis shoes without the laces.

"Why don't you get dressed and come with me to Lotaburger for a hamburger?" my mom asked.

"Nah," I said, "but you can bring me something back."

"Come with me," she said. "Come on, I'm taking Bella. You don't even need to get out of the car."

I sighed. I had had enough of the world for that day. Plus I hadn't showered in three or four days, and I smelled. I hated the shower, hated going into the bathroom. Too many triggers in there. Normally I would have continued to say no, but I wanted to appease my mom, who had been pressuring me to do something, to get a job and move on in my life. It had been five months since I'd planted myself in Mimi's back house, and I was going nowhere, physically *or* psychologically.

"Okay," I said, "but I'm not getting dressed, and I'm definitely not getting out of the car."

"Fine."

My mom drove, as usual. I sat in the passenger seat and Bella slept in the back. As soon as we backed out of the drive, I saw a cop pull behind us.

"They're coming to arrest me," I said.

"Don't be so paranoid, Alli," my mom said. "MPD would let us know if anything was going to happen."

"I'm not being paranoid," I said.

"It's been months. If they were going to do something, they would have done it by now. It's probably just a traffic cop." I saw her glance at the speedometer.

The patrol car followed us for about two miles. I knew they were looking for a safe place to stop us, one where I wouldn't be able to run. About ten minutes passed and they lit us up. My mom carefully pulled over.

"I don't think I was going too fast," she said. "Must be a brake light out or something."

"Trust me, Mom, they're here for me."

An officer approached the car, a female patrol cop. Then I absolutely knew it was for me—they would need a female to pat me down.

The cop motioned for my mom to open the window.

"We'd like to see your ID," she said. My mom fumbled with her purse.

"Not yours," the officer said, pointing to me. "Hers."

"I don't have any ID on me," I said.

At that time, about five unmarked patrol cars surrounded us. I suppose they thought I was going to flee, but there I was in my pajamas.

My mom's look of fear imprinted on my brain. I vowed, *I will never hurt her like this again.*

Meanwhile, the cop was eyeing Bella in the backseat. "Is that dog dangerous?" she asked.

"No, she's fine," I said, and looked back at Bella, still sound asleep through all the commotion.

Five plainclothes officers in tactical gear approached the car. Did they think I was going to be armed? Although they didn't draw down on me, they were obviously expecting the worst.

"Step out of the car, Miss Moore," one of the plainclothes cops said, a huge guy, very intimidating.

I did, feeling strangely calm. My mom was on the verge of tears, but I guess my cop skills of calm under duress were in full effect.

"We're placing you under arrest," he said, and read me my rights. "Do you know what you're getting arrested for?"

"I'm sure it's drug-related," I said.

The female cop patted me down and placed me in the back of her patrol car. I was numb. I didn't cry, but I felt terrible for my mom. They asked her to leave the scene, and she did.

The big guy who had asked me to step out of the car came and sat with me in the back of the patrol car.

"So, you're being arrested for multiple crimes," he said. "You look like a nice girl. How did this all happen?"

I gave him one word: "Meth."

He nodded and got out of the car, and then another guy, a vice cop, came in, interrogating me about drugs in Albuquerque. I don't know what MPD had told these guys, or what they thought about my drug connections, but they seemed to think I had information on the cartels there.

"Listen," I said, "I've been sober for six months. I have no clue about the smallest amount of drug running in New Mexico."

"You aren't using anymore?" he asked, sounding disappointed.

I shook my head. They had expected me to be tied into the rough West Central drug scene, but instead they found a sober girl in her pajamas being dragged out for lunch with her mom.

I wanted to be helpful, so I said, "When I was using, the way I found drugs in Washington was through Craigslist. The dealers advertise. If you want to start a new and different investigation, you should utilize the Internet."

He nodded, and then it was time to go. They transported me to the Albuquerque metro station downtown, where I was put in a holding cell.

Minutes later, I was on a transport bus with five other girls. The van was small and had no air conditioning; the girls were rowdy and defiant, all misdemeanor women claiming they were innocent and APD was corrupt. They were ghetto, and I fit in just fine. I was still in my duct-taped pajamas and not looking very good.

One of the girls said, "What smells?"

"Me," I said.

After that, the girls left me alone as we traveled to the Metropolitan Detention Center, the county jail thirty minutes outside Albuquerque. When we got there, we were strip-searched and showered. I really did smell, so the shower was a good thing.

In my first orange jumpsuit, I was able to call my mom from the intake waiting area. I told her what I had been told: my charges were in warrant form, and we would be able to see them soon. And one more thing: my bail was set for $150,000.

I was glad I didn't have to see her face when I delivered that number to her. She had spent all her savings and then some on rehab. There was no money left for bail.

I stayed in the Albuquerque prison for two weeks, waiting for MPD to come get me. Like all cops in prison, I was put in protective custody to keep me from the regular inmates. I held up pretty well, except that for the first several days, I had no meds. I had been skeptical about my antihallucinogenic drugs up to that point, but after my first night without them I realized that they really did work.

MPD had investigated me deeply. My police report was more than eight hundred pages long. There were copies of emails between the dealer and me, and between Keawe and me; there were phone records, medical records, a report all the way back to my abortion two and a half years earlier.

I was facing twenty-five felony counts. Many were drug possession and evidence tampering; some were forgery; others were related to claiming sick leave through the leave-sharing program, and monetary benefits. Erin's fund-raiser. Many of the counts ended with the words "by deception."

While I sat in jail, my mom arranged everything. A lawyer in Maui. A temporary place to live. A bail bondsman for the $150,000, which she could only get by putting up Mimi's house as collateral. I felt horrible about that, but it was all that was left.

My mom believed I could not remain sober on my own, so without even discussing it with me, she made plans to go to Hawaii with me. For as long as it took. She flew over before I did to arrange bail.

I was transported to Maui in handcuffs and leg irons on a commercial flight. Detective Keopu and another detective I had once worked with, Sergeant Lloyd, accompanied me. They were courteous and respectful, trying to give me words of encouragement along the way, but I was so ashamed I could barely look at them.

When I stepped off the plane in Maui, two officers I didn't know were waiting for me. Everyone in the airport stared. I felt like a freak show, like Hannibal Lecter.

I was crying so hard I couldn't see. I put my head down and tried to take one step after another. Keopu and Lloyd were on either side of me, guiding me, holding me up. My impulse was flight—but the leg irons and cuffs made that impossible. I had to face these officers, and they took me directly to the station.

I was momentarily comforted by the smell of the station. It was so familiar, homelike, but then I faced the mirrored glass of the receiving desk. I felt like the entire station was behind the glass watching me, all my brothers and sisters in blue looking at me with hate in their eyes, judging me, and having every right to do so. Was Keawe there? Erin? I had no idea who or how many people were behind the glass or watching from dispatch or seeing me on the cameras, but in my mind I was facing all of them. My physical anxiety, fear, shame, guilt, and remorse rose and filled all the available space. It hit me for the first time: the gravity of what I had done and the hurt I had inflicted on the whole department. The whole island.

I hadn't cried when I was arrested or when I was in general population at Metro, but now I began to weep hysterically. The tears were uncontrollable, and there was no one to comfort me, nowhere even to turn my head. It was one of the worst moments of my life.

I wanted to plead guilty immediately, to tell everyone, "Yes, yes, I did these terrible things," and be put away forever. The lawyers advised me differently. They wanted a not-guilty plea first.

I only spent one night in jail in Maui. My mom posted bail, and I entered my plea the next day. I wasn't allowed to leave the state of Hawaii, but they did let me transfer from Maui to Oahu to await trial and sentencing. I was grateful for that. Having to stay on Maui and risk seeing all the people I had hurt would have been unbearable. It was bad enough seeing my picture in the newspapers and on the nightly news. Because I was a cop, mine was a high-profile case.

My mom had rented an apartment on the fourteenth floor of a high-rise building in Honolulu. Knowing my fear of footsteps above me, my mom had tried to get the top floor but settled for an apartment with an empty unit above it. Often I walked up and down the fourteen flights of stairs because I was afraid to be in an elevator with a man.

The apartment building had an enormous mural of a whale on the side and overlooked the Ala Wai Canal. I picked up smoking for a while and often sat on the lanai with a cigarette, watching people go up and down the canal or walk along the sidewalks on either side of it. I settled into a routine of waiting—for pretrial hearings that got postponed, for meetings with lawyers that always left me in tears. Waiting. Just waiting.

Much as I wanted to, in Oahu there was no way I could continue to hide from life. My bail conditions demanded that I do many things that kept me in the real world. First and foremost, I had to find a job. My bail bondsman thought he could get me work in his office, but that didn't pan out. I couldn't face waitressing, so I turned to retail. I put in applications everywhere, but it was difficult to find work because I had to disclose my arrest status. I did manage to get interviews at Pier 1 and Victoria's Secret, and Victoria's Secret hired me. As a salesperson I was supposed to increase women's self-esteem, and yet I myself had none. It felt cruel and almost comical to be hired by a store whose purpose was to make women feel good about their bodies while I felt like dirt.

27

Ironically, rehab had left me with no self-knowledge at all—just more avoidance—but being arrested pointed me in the direction of the understanding I needed. When I thought about what I had done to all my colleagues, I was filled with remorse. I had been afraid to face them, but suddenly I craved the opportunity to look them in the eyes and say I was sorry. I started writing out my thoughts, recording what I would say at my sentencing. I just wanted something good to come out of a terrible, terrible situation.

Meanwhile, I was struggling with my job at Victoria's Secret. I liked helping women find what they needed—it was gratifying—but the constant contact with the public made me uneasy. One day a woman approached the cash register, and when I asked, "Can I help you with anything?" she looked at me with suddenly furious eyes.

"You have some nerve," she said.

"I'm sorry? I—"

"Yeah, you are," she said. "You're a very *sorry* person." She launched into a verbal attack, berating me loudly, causing a scene, and I realized from what she was saying that she was an MPD dispatcher. I didn't recognize her—we never saw the dispatchers. They're cop groupies and love cops, except for the female ones.

If this woman I didn't even know hated me so much, what must my former friends think of me?

I was finally able to gather myself and walk away. But the scene with the dispatcher caused a ruckus, and my managers took notice.

Apparently, word spread through MPD, and just a week later, Keawe's wife came into the store. Of course I recognized her instantly.

"Who do you think you are?" she asked me. "You say you're an addict, but I don't believe it. I've seen addicts before and they never did anything like this. You're a sociopath. Do you know you're going to prison for years and years? I hope you do!" She stood inches away from me, screaming at me in the middle of the store.

"Look," I said quietly, "I get that you hate me."

"You're crazy!" she said. "You're a liar. That abortion is a lie!"

I couldn't believe it. Keawe was still denying our affair to his wife.

"Why don't you check the court records?" I asked.

That took her aback. She paused for a moment and then said, "You leave us alone, you bitch. You're a stalker."

Someone I worked with came up, and Colleen left angrily, but my managers put me on leave. They were understanding, but they couldn't have displays like that going on in the store. It looked like I was going to be fired, but my probation officer was supportive, and the attorneys contacted MPD. The end result was that I still had a job, and Keawe was told to keep his wife away from me.

I was taken off the floor. I started working after hours, revamping and stocking, and that was better for me. I was grateful that I didn't have to see any customers. No men except for my supervisor, and he was a gay Asian man. I was okay with Asian men, Hawaiian men, African-American men, but every time I walked by a white middle-aged man, I would think about stabbing him or setting him on fire.

Every day was a complete and utter struggle not to use. The nights were worse. I could never sleep, and the flashbacks tormented me. Some nights I felt sure I would hurl myself off the lanai onto the asphalt fourteen stories below. I started to open up to my mom a little bit about the flashbacks, the dealer. Because we were living in such close quarters, I couldn't hide anything from her. It was time for her to know, and she deserved to know. Bit by bit, I began to tell her some of what the dealer had done to me.

"My God, Alli, that man is still out there," she said. "We need to press charges. We need to make sure he's not doing this to someone else. We need to—"

I stopped her. I knew how the law worked. "It's my word against his, Mom," I said, "and I'm an addict facing felony charges. Who's going to believe me? There's no evidence."

"But they can get evidence. If they get a warrant, they'll find the drugs and all those cameras and—"

"They can't get a warrant on my word alone. You can't just accuse someone of doing drugs or some other crime and obtain a warrant."

"But your testimony—"

"My testimony?" I felt anger coursing through my body. Anger not at my mom but at the situation the dealer had put me in. "My testimony? Even if they could somehow obtain a warrant and recover the evidence, who would actually be on trial? Me, Mom. I'm a discredited witness."

"That man needs to be punished for what he's done," my mom said.

"You're too naïve, Mom. It doesn't work that way. It's about evidence and the law. Of all people, I know that best."

"I know, sweetie," my mom said, backing off. "You've just been through so much."

My mom was my rock during this time. When I couldn't stay sober for myself, I stayed sober for her. She held up well, she was strong. She had to be. She felt she was responsible for keeping me alive.

My mom was a beautiful, amazing woman who deserved better. The life she lived belonged to another. She deserved a better husband, a better daughter, more loving parents. She deserved to wear better shoes. Yes, shoes. Everything she was, had, and could ever possibly be had been given away to friends and family. Her shoes were always worn and old. Never name-brand. She had carried me, and other friends and family, on her shoulders. I could see that in her shoes.

I broke this woman, I hurt her so deeply, so painfully. She would never admit it, or even face the truth about my horrendous actions against her, but it's the truth. I knew how she would die, and my sister agreed. My mother would die from a broken heart. My father cracked it, I shattered it, and my sister was forever trying to fix it. I knew one day that heart would stop, and when it did, I would lose all that was good in my life.

I knew I couldn't survive without my mother. My main motivation was to turn into the daughter she believed I was, to salvage the time I had left with her, to find a way to someday laugh with her and take care of her, emotionally and financially.

One of the therapists I was seeing in Oahu called it "a fucking wonderment" that I had remained sober this long. I began to think it was my survival instinct—the instinct that made me a good cop, the instinct that got me out of that house—because I knew the only way to survive was to stay sober. If I used again, I would die.

In August, I decided to change my plea from not guilty to guilty. I had wanted to plead guilty right from the beginning, and now my lawyers agreed. I knew I couldn't live through a trial, and I wanted to own up to what I had done, to make amends. After that, I waited for my sentencing date. Waited to see if I would go to prison. Waited to see if I could stay sober through all of it.

And then finally the waiting was over. I had a sentencing date of October 29. We had to fly to Maui for it, and the night before we left, my mom and I made dinner and sat on the lanai, watching the sunset. I didn't know if I would be coming back to this apartment. If I got probation, I would have to stay in Maui until the terms were worked out. If I was sentenced to time, I would be sent straight to jail.

I stared down at the canal below, at the people who drifted by in the early evening. Even from this far up, I could easily identify the drug dealers who passed by below.

I watched one man, a middle-aged white man, waiting for two tiny pretty Asian women to cross the street to him. They were agitated and fluttery, and he was loudly angry about something. He was dressed in black, with cheap chains dangling from his soft hips and a too-tight shirt open low. He was sleazy, a wannabe bad boy like he'd seen in MTV videos. I instantly hated him and worried for the girls. If I had a firearm, I would have taken aim at him from above.

In my other life, my life as a cop, I could have done something to defuse the situation. But now I was helpless. I could only look down, see him for the power he had, and feel angry that the girls wouldn't get away from him.

But they needed him. They needed his drugs.

He had them, and he knew it.

I worried that Keawe's wife might show up at my sentencing hearing. I also secretly hoped Keawe would be there.

But on the day of my sentencing, no one at all was there. Just my mom and the lawyers and a couple of reporters.

My lawyer argued that the PTSD, the addiction, and the lifelong loss of my shield should be taken into account when sentencing me—that, in effect, I was already being punished enough. I was hoping for probation only; the prosecutor was angling for five years in prison.

I barely made it through my prepared statement, which was a heartfelt apology to my friends, my family, the MPD, and the county of Maui in general.

"MPD gave me the opportunity to have an amazing career," I told the judge, "and I provided far less than my best. The betrayal I have imposed upon them will forever haunt me. I know great shame. I am overcome with remorse, and a spoken apology seems frail compared to the gravity of my actions."

I had worked on that statement for days and meant every word of it. I only wished the people who needed to hear it had been there.

The judge asked me what I thought my sentence should be.

"Probation," I answered. "I think jail is the wrong place for addicts." From what I'd seen from my time in jail in Albuquerque, I knew how available drugs were. I was worried for myself in that environment. Worried for any addict.

28

Moana grew up in the projects on Oahu. Exposed to narcotics from birth, she was raised to believe in three kinds of law enforcement: police officers, cops, and pigs. *Police officers* were the heroes that pulled you from a burning vehicle. *Cops* were the ones that responded to 911 calls. And *pigs*, which included the majority of law enforcement, were those that slapped you around, "taxed" you, and took your dope.

"You never, ever talk to or run to any of the three," she told me.

Moana, a Samoan, was one of the girls in the Federal Detention Center on Oahu. Her sentencing date was coming up, and I was helping her write a letter to her judge.

"I still can't believe I'm talking to a cop," she told me.

At first, I had been worried about what the women in prison would think of me. Like Moana, many of them were raised to fear and hate the police, and even though I was an inmate just like them, no one could ever forget I was also a cop.

As a former cop, a former *vice* cop, a *haole* female who not only broke the law but also hurt the people she loved in the most heinous way, I felt I should be getting my ass kicked in prison on a daily basis. I should have been in the hole because general population was too dangerous for me. I should have gotten no support from the guards or compassion from the staff. That was how prison should be for cops, a consequence of abusing the responsibility and trust given to them.

But that's not how it was for me. The girls accepted me and treated me well. I liked them. The majority of the women in the FDC were bright and articulate. It was easy for me to forget I was housed with some very seasoned manipulators, liars, and thieves. Even easier for me to forget that I was one of them.

One of the first friends I made in the FDC was Bets, a *tita* from Maui, in for selling drugs and stabbing her husband. On my third day there, she sat down to eat breakfast with me.

"You the Maui cop?" she asked. I could tell by her face she already knew that I was.

I nodded. I figured we'd get into a fight and I'd be sent to solitary. She was masculine with a football player's shoulders. She was going to destroy me.

Instead, she laughed. "I was one of Patrick's first informants on Molokai," she said. "Way back when."

"Really?" I said. "So you know all the vice guys."

"I know 'em," she said, and started rattling off names and details about a bunch of my old friends. She remembered a lot of them, even though she had already been in for eight years.

"You know I'm in the cell above you in three Alpha, right?" she asked.

"No," I said. "I didn't."

"You woke me up last night," she said accusingly.

"Oh," I said. I had had a horrible flashback during the night and ran into my cell wall trying to get away from the dealer. "I'm sorry."

"I heard a big crash," she said.

"I ran into the wall." I tried to be nonchalant. "Must have been a nightmare."

"And you ran into a wall?"

"I guess I did."

"Well, why'd you do that?" she laughed. "I'm gonna call you 'Wally.'"

I laughed. If a nickname was all I got from her, things were going to be okay.

"Why do you have your own cell anyway?" she asked.

"I'm not sure," I said, though I knew. It was the PTSD, the flashbacks. They couldn't put me in with another inmate if I was going to be hallucinating and crashing into walls in the middle of the night. Too dangerous for both of us.

"Where they got you working?" Bets asked me.

"The kitchen."

"Not bad, but they mix state and federal bodies there, and you gotta watch out for the state bodies."

"So far I like it," I said, but she was right. The state prisons were full, so many of the state criminals got sent to the FDC. It could get touchy with the state girls. They tended to be the low-level criminals, the fighters.

Things went fine for me in the kitchen for about a month. Then a new girl came in, a girl I had arrested for selling drugs a couple of years earlier in Lahaina. She recognized me immediately and came at me swinging. Luckily, the guard broke it up, and soon I had a new job as athletic director.

Compared to Washington, prison was amazing. Almost empowering, which sounds insane. Since my sentencing, I had come to realize that I had survived Washington and achieved sobriety by choice, not by circumstance. After the magnitude of my actions, my addiction, and the circumstances that followed, I couldn't believe I was still breathing. Some days I woke up unable to comprehend that I was in prison—*prison!*—but the fact that I even woke up was amazing.

Nights were a different story. That was when the PTSD struck. I lived and breathed my nights, and sometimes they were unbearable. During the day I still had flashbacks where I was paralyzed by fear, but I couldn't explain to the guard, "I can't do this task because I'm hallucinating a drug dealer coming after me." I had to function and live through them, and that seemed to make me stronger.

Drugs were not an issue for me in prison. It is very difficult to smuggle contraband into federal prison. Cell phones and cigarettes, yes, but because the others looked at me as a narc, if there were drugs, I never knew about them.

I did find myself wanting to use in prison, but not meth. I wanted drugs to help me sleep, to make me not feel or think, to numb me out. Something like heroin. It would have been a nightmare to be on tweaker time in a prison cell.

After six months of incarceration, I was made head orderly of the unit, which meant I got paid the most next to the commissary girls. I ran the daily functions and maintenance of the unit, everything from roster assignments to the unit orderlies' payroll.

I was grateful for my job. All inmates wore the same color, but the girls called me the "boss." When I politely told them, "I'm not the boss. I only take care of unit sanitation," they responded, "Okay, boss."

How I got myself in this position in six months I had no idea.

The head orderlies in the men's units? They were the biggest badass drug dealers in Hawaii. They ran shit and had a massive amount of power even while incarcerated. I was so far from that.

But I did fill a void in our unit. I made the girls laugh initially, and then I gained their trust by keeping my mouth shut and my ears open. They entrusted me with their letters to judges, their communications with lawyers.

In prison, my thoughts turned to Keawe more than I would like to confess. I knew I could never contact him again, though I did think about it. I composed letters to him in my head all the time. Every song related to him, every conversation triggered a memory I had forgotten during my drug abuse. Despite all that, I regretted that we were ever together. It had been nearly two years since I'd seen him, but since the day I arrived at the dealer's house for the last time, I felt as though time had stopped. My love for Keawe, my anger, regret, despair, and grief—all these emotions were fresh to me, and I clung to them because I knew Keawe would be the last man I could love. I hated men now, raged against them in my thoughts, plotted to kill them in my dreams.

I wasn't in touch with Keawe in prison, but he had friends who were prison guards, and once a guard came up to me and told me Keawe was worried about me. Did I need anything? he asked. Could he get me anything? I was so paranoid about being set up by the guards that I just walked away. Some guards were dirty, but others guards would just test you to see if you would accept contraband. I didn't want to take that chance either way.

In prison I felt safe enough to rage at Washington. I wanted to torture the dealer. I wanted to burn down that house. I found myself dreaming about how I would take my vengeance against the man.

I also had a few using dreams. I almost welcomed them; they

were a break from the nightmares and PTSD, though almost as traumatic. I always woke up terrified that I had relapsed, and for a brief moment I found solace in the fact that I was in prison in a controlled environment.

Prison is a violent place, and loud and cold, but my responsibilities were lined out for me there. It was easy to follow the rules. And in some ways, prison is cushy. We had pillows, TV, books, and a gym. There was MTV. Zumba classes. Email. You could have ramen noodles and coffee at the commissary. Yet when your cell door closed, you remembered what got you there.

My body ached from sleeping on steel, but the structure and control kept me safe enough to confront my past. In my awakening, I felt I could not move forward in my life without telling my story. I needed to expel my past before I could construct some sort of future.

29

I served my full twelve months at the FDC and was released at the end of October.

Keawe emailed me the day I got out. He wanted to meet me, but I ignored his email. My mom quit her job in New Mexico once again and flew to be with me in Oahu while I petitioned to serve my five years probation in New Mexico. The two of us stayed in a hotel room waiting for my parole to be transferred. I couldn't wait to get out of the state of Hawaii.

It was time to go home.

I moved back to Albuquerque in early December, when everything in New Mexico was brown and scrubby and ugly. These dead winters were one of the main reasons I had fled to Maui in the first place, but now the lush and green island would never be my home again. I intended never to go back.

I moved into Mimi's back house with my mom and started

working for the parents of one of my mom's friends. As a convicted felon, I found it hard to get a regular job, so I was grateful for a full-time position with a couple in their eighties. I cooked their meals, did their shopping, and drove them to appointments and social engagements.

Being a full-time caretaker taught me patience and forced me into public situations that I would have avoided if given a choice. I began to learn compassion. I learned to help someone else. I had fucked up so badly that all I wanted to do was help others.

Once I was safely in New Mexico, I returned Keawe's email. He emailed me back, but by then I had started seeing my therapist and opted to delete his email from my inbox before reading it. I also blocked his email address. After all the hurt our relationship caused, I couldn't believe either of us was willing to be in contact. I needed to make it stop. He would remain, like my father, a man in my life who couldn't, or wouldn't, love me enough.

My life stayed very small, again by choice. I saw my family and the family of the couple I worked for. My sister had kept her distance for a long time, but we slowly began to communicate again. My heart thrilled every time I got a text message from her; I lived for Skype conversations with my little nieces. I had not seen them since leaving Washington, and I had not seen my sister since rehab. I could not go to Washington, but my hope was that they would one day decide to visit us in New Mexico.

In my free time, which by choice was not much, I tried to learn how to play guitar. However, the meth had messed with my brain and my retention was pretty poor. I often found myself just trying to make pretty sounds.

I spent a lot of time with my dog Bella and Tater, my brand-new mastiff puppy. Life was simple and quiet and I liked it that way.

On Sundays, my one day off, I developed a ritual with my mom.

In the mornings, we would drive out to a coffee shop on the west side and then take a drive through the gorgeous valley and talk about the week. We would text my sister and compare this Sunday's coffee to the last week's and have a great time. Then we would come home and go our separate ways. I would try to do something productive but would often end up wandering around the house, starting small projects that I would never finish. Later, we would grab Mimi and have a wonderful lunch somewhere, usually at Little Anita's because it was Mimi's favorite. We would talk about the past week, what was new in the art world and with the family, and what was going on in my job.

What I was most proud of was that with my job I was able to support my mom. Since she was able to stay home and work on her artwork full-time, I could finally help her live out her dream. On hard days, the thought that I could give back to my family got me through. I started to find my way back to who I always believed I was in my heart. It was a long journey and not easy.

I started uncovering new layers of emotions in therapy. It was almost easier when I was in prison and when I had just been released because then I was just trying to get through my day, function, do what I had to do to meet my probation requirements. Now, as I worked more on the PTSD, my mind constantly returned to the past. Sometimes I felt my days were just logged hours waiting for the nights.

The guilt at times was crippling, paralyzing, and I spent a lot of time thinking about my friends, wondering what they were doing and how they were doing. Staying busy seemed to be the only thing to combat my racing thoughts while I worked in therapy to ease the guilt and pain of what I had done. The PTSD was wearing. I tried to accept my PTSD for what it was. I found that if I got my hopes up for a little improvement or a new medication, the disappointment was almost too much to bear. I started focusing mostly on how to live with it. When my therapist introduced me to eye movement desensitization and reprocessing (EMDR) therapy, often used to treat Iraq vets and other victims of PTSD, I got excited at first. I mistakenly thought it erased your memories, but it merely teaches you how to live with them.

Despite the PTSD, I still found myself having meth cravings. They pissed me off more than scared me, but the cravings still haunted me. I could go months without having dreams of using and then suddenly notice how healthy my veins looked. That always led to a craving.

My old thoughts of making amends, of rectifying my past faded a bit. I wanted to apologize to everyone I'd hurt, but I didn't feel I had the right to enter their lives and selfishly apologize. The more I faced my past in therapy, the more I realized my actions inflicted irrevocable pain and damage not only on those I loved but also on myself. Each day, making the right choices, working hard but finding balance, seemed like the only option for me.

I began to feel youthful again. I had felt so old in rehab and in prison, and my bones always hurt, but now I was excited about my future and what it might hold. I was thinking about taking college classes or starting my own business. Under the terms of my parole, I couldn't leave Albuquerque's Bernalillo County for three more years, but after that I was hoping to travel.

Despite my progress, the sacrifices I made for drugs are everlasting. The memories I have of that house are everlasting. If I could have gotten a lobotomy or some sort of procedure to take them away, I would have. But I couldn't. I could only learn to live with them.

What occurred in that house scarred me so deeply that some days breathing seemed impossible. Had I been sober and had any sort of clarity when I was there, I wouldn't have survived. The mental pain would have eaten my body to death. The meth gave me a false sense of reality, masking the truth and keeping me alive until it almost killed me. The dealer stole my life, tattooed my mind with memories that I could not remove.

I was happy for my second chance. It taught me that everything is a survivable situation. I lost myself fully, yet even now I have a chance at a life.

Still, I miss my life on Maui. I miss my job, the work, my supervisors. I miss the adrenaline, I miss my desk, and I miss composing affidavits and warrants, of all things. I miss the investigation, trying to figure out the drug lines, the imports and exports, where the dope is hidden. I miss the technology and the surveillance. I miss the laughs at the station, the inappropriate dirty jokes and profane emails. I miss feeling at home in an all-male environment, when I didn't despise men and think of lighting them on fire or stabbing them to death. I miss cleaning my firearms, I miss the radio, the constant chatter of the patrolmen working the beat. I miss learning the new laws, the techniques, the slang, and latest narcotics news. I miss the integrity I used to have. I miss the friendships.

I know I threw all these things away the day I did that first line of ice, when I didn't even know that I should smoke it or how to smoke it. And like anyone who has cast their lot in life, who has made choices—by which I guess I mean any human being—I have had to learn to live with them. I've learned to get up each morning, go to work, look forward to Sunday coffees with my mom and walks with my dogs and precious phone conversations with my sister and the particular way the wide New Mexico sky gives me room to move forward in my life.

I often think of the words Sergeant Mankell, my recruit school combat instructor, wrote to me in a letter on the day of graduation:

You have the heart of a lion, and you never quit.
You acknowledged your pain, but did not indulge it.
You are gentle and humble, yet sharp as a sword.
You remained generous in all that I have seen you do.
You are a warrior.

On my best days, I believe those words still apply.
I never intended to be a cop.
I never imagined I'd be an addict.
By thirty years old, I had been both.

Acknowledgments

Allison Moore

I would like to express my gratitude to the many people who saw me through this book, past to present.

To my aunt Stella Krauss, without whom this book would not have been written: thank you for your endless support, careful attention, and humor.

I'd like to thank Nancy Woodruff, whose patience, hard work, love, and understanding have forever changed my life.

I would also like to thank Jason Anthony and Maria Massie at Lippincott Massie McQuilkin and Stacy Creamer and Miya Kumangai at Touchstone for their help in creating, editing, and publishing this book.

My deepest appreciation goes to Daniel Clothier, Ed Curran, Ti, Dr. Ritchie, Mike, Steve, Shelly, Nicole, and the entire staff at Vista Taos Renewal Center. Without your dedication and commitment, I would not be here today.

To Andrew Martin, Robert Rivera, and Charles Fisher: thank you so much for your help and patience.

Thank you to Dr. Laura M. Sturgis.

To Dr. Jane Bloomfield: thank you for believing in me and being the absolute catalyst for this journey. To Leslie Lindquist: thank you for your countless hours of counseling and support and friendship.

Thank you to Lynn Hopkins. I couldn't have gotten this far without you.

To Carolyn Mason: thank you for giving me critical opportunities, support, faith, and encouragement. You have been my lifeline. To Bill C. Carroll: thank you for believing in me.

To Kristy Anderson: thank you for being unwavering in your support.

Sonia Grace: thank you for always reminding me of my greater purpose.

To Mrs. Francelynn Lum and Lydia Hockridge: thank you for all your help, guidance, and encouragement.

To Kathy Hall, LISW, and Jered Ebenrek, words can't express my thoughts: thank you.

Thank you to Honorable Judge R. Bissen: your words at sentencing continue to follow me daily.

Billy: thank you for sharing your joy and your outrageous laugh.

Dawn Freeze: thank you for being so accepting and such a supportive friend from the beginning.

To the Maui Police Department and all of the people I love, to those I hurt and those who were victimized by my actions: thank you for taking me into your family, for giving me your unconditional love, and for providing me with opportunities that I could not have imagined in my wildest dreams. I am deeply sorry. I think of you often, my Hawaiian family, and not a moment goes by that I do not miss you all.

To Detective Kaya, Detective Juan, Detective Dodds, and Sergeant Sagawinit: thank you for your compassion. You are my heroes. To my two closest friends at MPD: thank you for your friendship and love.

Above all, I would like to thank my courageous grandmother Billie/Mimi, Uncle Rick, Uncle Toby, Aunt Alison, Uncle Kurt, Uncle Bud, and Aunt Liz, who supported me through grinding financial demands as well as carried me emotionally and physically through seemingly endless challenges. Also, thanks to Uncle Jay, Aunt Rosie, my dear cousins, and extended family for their strength, their belief in me, their unconditional love, and for supporting and encouraging me despite the hurt I inflicted upon them. It has been and continues to be a long and difficult journey for them.

To my incredible mother: your heart drives me to be a better person. You are a daughter's greatest gift. Thank you.

To my sister: your love fuels my passion for life, your courage and support remain my anchor as well as my guiding light. For my brother-in-law, who helped and supported me even during the worst of times and forgave me for causing them: you inspire me. Thank you.

I would also like to say a special thank-you to my cousin Ryan. May his spirit continue to shine for all of us who struggle and help remind us that there is hope.

My apologies to anyone I may have failed to mention. Every person has been vital and key to my being here today. I want you to know I will always hold you dear to my heart. Thank you all.

Nancy Woodruff

All thanks for this book begin with Stella Krauss, former roommate and traveling companion, who introduced me to Alli's story and then to Alli. Heartfelt thanks also go to Jason Anthony and Maria Massie for immediately recognizing that Alli's story needed to be told and for helping in every way possible to make that happen. Charlotte and Phil Reavis, my aunt and uncle, offered wonderful hospitality during my research visit to Hawaii, and Alli's family and friends welcomed me as one of their own during my trip to New Mexico. My stalwart writer friends Sara Eckel, Renee Bacher, Anne Korkeakivi, and Camilla Trinchieri gave me sound advice and support throughout the writing of this book, and Fred Carl was instrumental in helping obtain important court records. Stacy Creamer and Miya Kumangai at Touchstone are gifted publishing professionals and a pleasure to work with. My family—Mark, Sage, Reed, and Owen Lancaster—always cared and always listened. Finally, I thank Allison Moore for sharing her story with me; Alli, working with you was an unexpected and remarkable gift, and your friendship and trust have enriched my life immeasurably.

About the Authors

Allison Moore is a former narcotics officer with the Maui Police Department. A native of New Mexico, she served a one-year sentence in the Federal Detention Center in Oahu for drug-related felonies. She is currently attempting to make amends to all those she has hurt and find her way back to life.

Nancy Woodruff received her MFA from Columbia University, and she has taught writing at Columbia; SUNY Purchase; Richmond, the American International University in London; and New York University. She is the author of two novels, *My Wife's Affair* and *Someone Else's Child*. She currently lives in Brooklyn with her husband, sons, and daughter.

"And whom do you think jails are for, Miss Moore?" the judge said.

"Violent offenders, Your Honor."

He looked at me thoughtfully for a moment. I had no idea what he was going to say. Then he started talking.

"The defendant was a con artist," he said. "She perpetrated a scam. She had a reason for her scam: she wanted drugs. She wanted to continue using drugs. She didn't want to give up her job, didn't want to ask for help from her family, who all appear quite willing and able to help."

As he talked about what he viewed as my calculated actions, my deceptions, I started to feel like I couldn't breathe.

He continued, "Miss Moore is such a convincing storyteller that the court can't tell if today is a continuation of that scam. Which Allison Moore is before us in court today? The Allison Moore that worked vice undercover, that was able to arrest and investigate drug dealers, or the other Allison Moore? The court understands the difficulty that vice officers have in having to live a double life, but at some point you went over and never came back."

Then, most painfully, he referred to a letter Erin Doyle had written against me. He said, "Miss Moore fooled an entire police department, as Miss Doyle says. She had every single person fooled. Eighty-eight officers donated their leave and time. Miss Doyle wrote a very strong letter detailing all the opportunities Miss Moore had to come clean to the person who was her confidant." I hadn't read the letter, but it wasn't hard to imagine how much Erin hated me. She had taken me in, taken care of me, and I had spit in her face.

Then he read the entire list of people who demanded restitution from me and the amounts I owed them.

I owed Officer Keawe Davis more than a thousand dollars.

The judge sentenced me to one year in prison and five years probation, beginning immediately.

I turned around, searching for my mom. She was right behind me, putting on a brave face, trying not to cry.

I knew what she was thinking. How could she keep me safe and sober while I was in prison?